G000058168

FAST FORWARD LEADERSHIP

How to exchange outmoded practices quickly for forward-looking leadership today

Louellen Essex

Mitchell Kusy

FINANCIAL TIMES

PRENTICE HALL

PEARSON EDUCATION LIMITED

Head Office:
Edinburgh Gate
Harlow CM20 2JE
Tel: +44 (0)1279 623623
Fax: +44 (0)1279 431059

London Office:
128 Long Acre, London WC2E 9AN
Tel: +44 (0)171 447 2000
Fax: +44 (0)171 240 5771

First published in Great Britain in 1999

ISBN 0 273 64201 4

British Library Cataloguing in Publication Data
A CIP catalogue record for this book can be obtained from the British Library.

10 9 8 7 6 5 4 3 2 1

Typeset by M Rules
Printed and bound in Great Britain by Biddles Ltd, Guildford & Kings Lynn

The Publishers' policy is to use paper manufactured from sustainable forests.

ABOUT THE AUTHORS
....

Dr Louellen Essex is President of her own leadership development consulting organization, Louellen Essex and Associates. Serving as an educator and consultant for over 17 years, her clients include a variety of corporations, governmental agencies, health care institutions and non-profit organizations, worldwide. She is an adjunct faculty member, Graduate School of Business, University of St Thomas, Minneapolis.

Dr Mitchell Kusy is Associate Professor and Chair, Graduate Department of Organization Learning & Development, University of St Thomas, Minneapolis. Previously, he directed the leadership and organization development areas in non-profit and Fortune 500 firms for 15 years. Named 1998 Organization Development Practitioner of the Year by the Minnesota Organization Development Network, he consults internationally in leadership development, strategic planning, and organizational change.

Dedicated to all the leaders who have encouraged us to write this book, contributed to it, and inspire others daily

CONTENTS

ACKNOWLEDGMENTS

Many people helped shape our thinking about leadership. To those leaders we profiled, quoted and interviewed, we thank you for sharing your wisdom with others and us. You have opened many doors and we are grateful.

Our agent, Laurie Harper of Sebastian Literary Agency, has been our primary coach throughout our book-writing adventure. We cannot thank her enough for her steadfast guidance, critique, and insight.

We are grateful to our colleagues at the University of St Thomas School of Education, Graduate School of Business, and the Center for Health and Medical Affairs who have encouraged us throughout this effort. We also acknowledge our students, who have helped us reflect on innovative leadership practices.

We appreciate the outstanding efforts of the editorial and marketing team at Financial Times Prentice Hall. Special appreciation goes to Pradeep Jethi, Elizabeth Truran, Penelope Allport, Claudia Orrell, and Iain Campbell.

To our special advisors, Richard Weatherman, Scott Vrchota, Paul Griffin, and Scott Hvidsten, who have often been heard saying, "Are they ever going to finish that thing?", we say thanks for your patience, prodding, and support.

We are grateful to our family and friends who have had to endure our endless "book reports". Thank you for not abandoning us!

Finally, to our clients who have allowed us to learn from them and their organizations, we acknowledge we couldn't have written this without you.

FOREWORD

Recently I was leading a session with the faculty of a major business school on the topic of leadership. During this session we brainstormed a myriad of qualities and characteristics relating to effective leadership. As expected, the group volunteered a wide range of attributes: vision, creativity, drive, charisma and motivation to mention a few. As we were in the process of finalizing our model of leadership, one of the professors boldly volunteered an interesting and somewhat surprising attribute to the mix: transcendence. I was so intrigued by his suggestion that I probed into what transcendence had to do with leadership. His response was direct and straightforward, "Leaders go beyond what is." The truth of his penetrating statement pierced through all the abstract models we had been creating.

Whether we are leading our lives, leading our work or leading our organizations, we are continually "going beyond what is." If we are not going beyond what is, we may be managing what is but not leading ourselves and others into the future.

What needs to be present at that crucial moment of authentic leadership that allows us to "go beyond what is?" As a result of coaching senior leaders of organizations at LeaderSource for the past 20 years, we have observed two essential qualities which need to be present: trust and knowledge.

At the moment of real leadership – when we are about to leap across a chasm from the known to the unknown – there is no guarantee of a successful landing or precedent to guide our vault. We may succeed; we may fail. What bridges us from the known to the unknown? Trust. Trust in ourselves that regardless of outcome we will endure. Trust that our planning and preparation have been sufficient. Trust in others that they have been prepared to do the right thing. Our ability to trust and let go of our current trapeze far before we have secured our hold on the next bar is deeply rooted in our personal qualities of character and courage. Leaders lead by virtue of who they are. Sometimes we need to deeply work on who we are so we can be more open to letting go of "what is" and trust ourselves to venture into "what could be."

However, trust without sufficient knowledge and competence can lead to foolhardy or even dangerous pursuits. As important as it is to deepen our self-knowledge and trust to enhance our leadership effectiveness, it is equally important to expand our knowledge of the context of leadership.

To "go beyond what is" is a lot easier if we are grounded in a sense of what may be coming. Therefore we need to have a vision which is deeply connected to the knowledge of our current and projected circumstances. What will the world of work look like? What will the workforce be like as less of it is employee based? What will the workplace be like as technology continues to proliferate? In *Fast Forward Leadership*, Essex and Kusy give us clear insights and tools to understand this context of leadership.

This book represents a real opportunity for you. Use it as a book and you will get some interesting perspectives. However, use it as a navigational guide and you will begin "to go beyond what is" and fast forward your leadership into the future, now.

Kevin Cashman
Author, *Leadership from the Inside Out*
CEO, LeaderSource, Minneapolis, Minnesota

BLAZING THE TRAIL TO FUTURE LEADERSHIP SUCCESS

YOUR TRACK TO FUTURE SUCCESS WON'T
BE FOUND ON PAST TRAILS

Think about how you lead now and how you led just five years ago. The same style? If you're like most leaders, there are no real differences between the two. Now, think about how you currently lead and compare this to how you will need to lead in the future. Any differences? We hope you are responding with a resounding "yes"! We have discovered that many of the typical leadership practices today will not work in the future – we're not talking the distant future, but soon. Even more critical, we have found that some of the ways you lead now may be largely ineffective because of the rapidly emerging new demands of the workforce, work, and workplace itself.

Consider this scenario. Megan Angeles, Vice-President of Marketing in a mid-sized food production company finds herself in a large private office, well-appointed, with an incredible skyline view, walnut desk, and book shelves – symbols of her success. By working long hours and demonstrating company loyalty, she has progressively worked her way up the organizational ladder. Megan has hired the most experienced, seasoned staff as her dedicated employees and designed clear job descriptions for them. Creating three functional teams reporting to her, she has had each focus on a set of defined products. This leader has applied the skills she learned in her MBA program and has wholeheartedly embraced participative management methods, holding regular meetings in the staff conference room to get individual and team input on decisions. She's introduced open cubicles for her entire staff and created more conference spaces for teams to work. Consistently motivating her staff via negotiating good pay raises and using a great deal of written praise, Megan also sends them to frequent training seminars to keep their skills up to date.

Can you find the outmoded concepts in this picture? Hint: there are ten. Megan is using behaviors that have previously been successful for her, expecting them to carry her into the future. This pattern is not likely to work because of emerging demands in the new work frontier. It's not that these practices should never be used in the future. What we're saying is that their effectiveness will be sharply reduced. Refer to Box 1.1 for a list of the ten obsolete leadership practices in this scenario. We have selected them to accentuate our point and stimulate your interest. If you're curious about why these concepts are outmoded, read on. We'll explore these and many others throughout this book as we explain what to stop and why, along with what to do instead. At the beginning of each chapter (3 through 9), we will present a scenario, related to a particular point that we have developed from a blend of the many obsolete practices in the workplace today. After each scenario, we'll alert you to what won't work, and then, focus on replacement strategies – what we refer to as *Fast Forward Leadership*.

➤➤ BOX 1.1   **Traditional leadership practices**

1 Private offices and cubicles
2 Movement up the ladder
3 Employees
4 Positions, jobs
5 Functional teams
6 Hard work yields success
7 Absolute participation
8 Offices, furniture as power symbols
9 Pay raises as incentives
10 Seminars as the standard training mode

While these concepts run rampant in many organizations, they will not be the tickets to future leadership success. Stay tuned for why these and many other concepts are outmoded; we'll help you understand what to do instead.

AVOID THE MIXED-MESSAGE PHENOMENON THAT BUSTS TRUST

One of the things we know from the gurus who study leadership practices is that successful leadership is about trust. The primary variable contributing to leader trust is reliability – predictable, consistent behavior.

Successful leaders are true to their words – their actions match what they say. When leaders hang on to old behaviors while espousing new ideas, those around them get confused and trust is eroded. Yet, many times, we have found they are unaware of how two conflicting sets of behaviors they display to others are diminishing their effectiveness.

> *When leaders hang on to old behaviors while espousing new ideas, those around them get confused and trust is eroded.*

OUR STUDY OF LEADERS WORLDWIDE

We discovered the *Fast Forward Leadership* concept as we engaged in an odyssey to find new shapes and forms of leadership. To understand better what leaders are doing now to position themselves and their organizations for ongoing success, we used the following approaches:

1 Discussions with innovative leaders worldwide

Over the past ten years, we have spoken with hundreds of successful leaders who appeared steps – and at times quantum leaps – ahead of their contemporaries. We began seeing common themes as they shared informally their insights with us at national and international conferences, during our consultations with them in their boardrooms and offices, and in leadership development seminars we conducted.

2 Research on current and anticipated leadership practices

We reviewed the current literature (1990–9) on organizational and leadership trends to determine what researchers and authors identified as critical factors needed for leadership success now and in the future.

3 Interviews with leaders worldwide in innovative organizations

We identified effective leaders in innovative organizations cited in the literature or selected from our own consulting practices. They represented a variety of organizational types including profit and non-profit; large-, medium-, and small-sized; service- and product-oriented. Using a structured interview format, we queried them about their current workforce characteristics, types of work and organizational designs they created, as well as the landscape of the workplace itself. We asked them about their current leadership actions, transitions anticipated, and their advice to other leaders.

At first, we wondered if these leaders would be willing to share the "secrets" of their success. We were pleasantly surprised to discover that every leader, bar none, wanted to convey anything that would help other leaders become more successful. They even opened doors for us to contact others in their own and other organizations – with a selfless "How may I help you?" attitude. They talked from their hearts, as well as their minds.

Our interviewees were from the following organizations:

- 3M
- ABB CE Nuclear Power
- American Express
- Andersen Consulting
- AT&T
- BMW
- California Department of General Services
- County of Los Angeles
- Dayton's Commercial Interiors
- Fallon-McElligott
- Forum Corporation
- KLM Royal Dutch Airlines
- Lawson Software
- Life USA Holding, Inc.
- Medtronic
- Minnesota Department of Health
- Minnesota Pollution Control Agency
- Motorola
- Northwest Area Foundation
- Norwest Banks
- Oracle Corporation
- Ridgeview Medical Center
- St Jude Medical

- Schneider Corporation
- Target Stores
- TCG
- Teltech
- Texas Refinery Corp.

We extracted the themes from our literature review and interviews, using them throughout this book to illustrate our key points.

THE *FAST FORWARD LEADERSHIP* CONCEPT

Fast Forward Leadership clarifies exactly what practices you should seriously consider eliminating from your repertoire and with what you should replace them. We have organized the following chapters into seven exchanges, reinforced by the lessons learned from our interviewees and research. These "exchanges" begin with Chapter 3:

Chapter 3: "The communication exchange: limited and informational for shared and persuasive;"

Chapter 4: "The workforce exchange: core and permanent for non-core and contract;"

Chapter 5: "The recognition exchange: single-generational for multi-generational focus;"

Chapter 6: "The team exchange: siloed and local for fluid and geographically dispersed;"

Chapter 7: "The development exchange: excessive team building for individual maverick appreciation;"

Chapter 8: "The workplace exchange: stationary edifices for mobile and virtual environments;"

Chapter 9: "The structure exchange: internally focused for externally partnered."

We consider *Fast Forward Leadership* to be a guidebook. In this frenetic age of just-in-time everything, leaders need a simple and sensible source they can go to for immediate help. We have compiled what

> *We encourage you to make these exchanges before it's too late – before others pass you by with innovative practices that leave you in the dust.*

we think you must know for your own career development as well as your organization's success. We encourage you to make these exchanges before it's too late – before others pass you by with innovative practices that leave you in the dust.

INSIGHTS FROM INNOVATIVE LEADERS

....

What they're doing and not doing today to prepare for tomorrow

....

I nnovative leaders are tossing out stale leadership practices as quickly as they are inventing new ones. Those we interviewed explained the forces propelling a need to change. They talked about their perceptions of the emerging workforce, types of work, and workplace, as well as what they are doing, and not doing, now to lead their organizations in the 21st century. This is what they told us.

SHIFTING INTO SIXTH GEAR

Why do organizations and their leaders need to change? Our interviewees placed technological advances on top of the list of trends driving organizational change. Increased access to information and the declining cost of technology has created a ripple effect impacting nearly every aspect of the way organizations do business. For example, Mike Stringer, Senior Vice-President of Adaytum Software (formerly Vice-President of International and Alliances at Lawson Software), described "disintermediation" as a recent development that takes the intermediary out of business interactions. Technology allows people to get information directly without going through a maze of clerks and vendors. He noted that one of his huge retailer-clients used the disintermediation strategy; they formerly had 80 accounts-payroll clerks answering questions from vendors to see if their invoices had been paid. Instead, they developed the Vendor Information System that gives a history of the invoice via the Internet, allowing for direct information access.

The leaders we interviewed spoke about economic conditions as another driving concern. In government, taxpayers are demanding cost effectiveness and, in organizations everywhere, leaner budgets are propelling the need for more efficiencies. Looming in the marketplaces surrounding the organizations that our leaders represent, competitors are on every corner, positioning themselves to grab market share and steal staff, particularly those with technological skills. Speed of product and service development, high-impact training, and information utilization and analysis become critical needs in this environment. And, the organizational playing field has expanded to include "global reach but local touch," said Glenn Gienko, Executive Vice-President and Director of Human Resources at Motorola, where 70 percent of the business is done outside the United States. More of an organization's business may be done internationally with people of many different cultures working together, using technology as their key linkage.

Our interviewees reported a clear change in staff-member values. Many new workforce entrants consider themselves "free agents," expecting to move frequently from organization to organization as their careers develop, remaining loyal only to those adequately meeting their needs. And with the demands of steadfast traditionalists (born before 1946), career-focused baby boomers (born 1946 through 1963), and independent generation Xers (born from 1964 through 1975), the desire for flexible work arrangements continues to soar (see also p. 77). Highly skilled technical staff, in particular, will be hard to retain if leaders don't build an adaptable work environment now, positioning their organizations as great places to work. Gillian Thomas, Human Resource Manager at Motorola Australia Software Centre, said, "In the preferred workplace of the future, and for younger workers in particular, work and home and fun are seamless." This is a concept that leaders must understand to begin decompartmentalizing their thinking about work.

Box 2.1 provides a complete listing of the trends to which our interviewees thought 21st-century leaders must be fully attuned.

▶▶ BOX 2.1   **Trends driving change**

- Technology links information to people.
- Customers raise their expectations: more speed, quality, and cost effectiveness.
- Talent becomes a critical competitive edge, yet hard to recruit and retain.
- Speed goes beyond product development to include training and information utilization.
- Staff members call out for balance in life.
- Workforce, work, and marketplace globalize.

These are the most frequently cited trends to which our interviewees thought 21st-century leaders must attune themselves.

THE CRESCENDO OF THE EXTERNAL WORKFORCE

Innovative leaders are positioning their organizations for an onslaught of non-core staff – temporary and contract. On the average, they predict a rapid increase, from 10 percent in 1997 to 25 percent in the year 2002, in the number of non-core staff their organizations would use (*see* Box 2.2). Correspondingly, they anticipate a decline in the percentage of internal, core staff members – from 90 percent to 75 percent. Essentially, this suggests a 150 percent increase in the number of non-core staff over five years.

►► BOX 2.2 **Average percentages of internal and external staff**

	Internal (core)	External (non-core)
1997	90%	10%
2002	75%	25%

In just five years, from 1997 to 2002, this is what leaders predicted would happen to the internal (core) and external (non-core) workforce. There is evidence from our leaders that these are very conservative estimates.

Temporary services have increased exponentially since the early 1980s, due to the demand organizations have for contingent staff. Typically, temporary staff are recruited, tested, screened, and employed by a firm which then places them on assignment in the host organization – the purchaser of the services. Or, a master vendor relationship might be developed where the temporary firm comes on-site to hire and place staff for a given organization. When the volume of placements is high, this type of arrangement reduces administrative costs and consolidates billing. Through our interviews, we found yet another model – the in-house temporary labor pool run as a "company-within-a-company" providing temporary staff on an as-needed basis.

Contract work, another alternative, is acquired through outsourcing in which organizations contract with external firms or individuals to perform an entire function within the organization; this may be limited to certain responsibilities or include entire departments. The progression of outsourcing in the past few years has been staggering. It is big business, as evidenced by the proliferation of outsourcing services and the fatter budgets organizations have devoted to this. Leaders report that some of the most significant benefits of outsourcing efforts include more effective service and lower costs than what could be accomplished with internal talent alone.

What are the key reasons organizations cite for using non-core staff? Some of the most common ones mentioned include cost reduction, increased flexibility, more effective service, and avoidance of the consequences of unnecessary layoffs during slack periods. Leaders we interviewed recognize the flexibility and efficiency they gain by being able to adjust quickly to market conditions and product or service demand. Gerhard Bihl, Director of Human Resources Policy and Strategy at BMW expressed the following perspective:

We get extra flexibility by "leasing" people. If down, we send them home. We don't have to fire and hire our own people. In extra good times, we lease employees.

WHAT'S IN A NAME?

We asked our interviewees what terminology they used to describe their non-core staff. Most commonly, this portion of the workforce is called contractors, temporaries, or consultants. Other terms we uncovered included vendors, as well as outsourced, and contingent staff (*see* Box 2.3). Karl Stauber, President of Northwest Area Foundation and former Undersecretary for Research, Education, and Economics at the US Department of Agriculture, uses one of the more unusual terms to describe non-core staff: "non-residential," indicating they do not work locally, on-site. At Lawson Software, Mike Stringer described use of the term "partner" to symbolize the shared role of both core and non-core staff in delivering total solutions to their customers. Gregg Steinhafel, Executive Vice-President of Merchandising at Target Stores, noted no special term for its non-core workforce; all staff are referred to as "team members." By blurring the lines of demarcation between internal and external staff, Target Stores promotes the concept that all staff are important.

> **➤➤ BOX 2.3** **Terms used to describe non-core staff**
>
> - Contractors*
> - Temporaries*
> - Consultants*
> - Vendors
> - Outsourced people
> - Temporary contract people
> - Contingent staff
>
> - Student assistants
> - Outside contractors
> - Out-of-house staff
> - Partners
> - Non-residential staff
> - Team members
>
> *The asterisked items are those most commonly mentioned for non-core staff.*

Innovative leaders with whom we talked are developing a vocabulary to describe their non-core staff in a way fitting their organizational culture. Clearly, a thoughtful approach now to the words used to describe this growing segment of the workforce will signal their place in the organization. Non-core staff may soon become the core, as their numbers bypass those of their core counterparts.

Non-core staff may soon become the core, as their numbers bypass those of their core counterparts.

WHO DOES WHAT?

Functions most suited for non-core positioning, said our interviewees, are technological, including systems analysis and maintenance, data management, computer programming, and software development. Administrative and marketing functions are also among those most often cited as good candidates for the non-core workforce to perform. Box 2.4 gives a complete listing of the tasks and functions our interviewees indicated are performed in their organizations by the non-core workforce.

The remaining work, done internally, should be centered on the organization's core competencies – what our interviewees determined, after careful analysis, was the real heart of their business. Innovative leaders are moving quickly now to help their organization determine what it does best and focus its energy there. However, this does not mean the non-core

> **►► BOX 2.4** **Tasks and functions performed by non-core staff**

Tasks	Functions
Technological*	Systems analysis and maintenance Data management Programming Software development
Administrative*	Mailroom processing Office support, clerical, secretarial Accounting
Marketing*	Telemarketing Customer service Advertising New product implementation Creative services Specialist roles Writing
Maintenance	Building maintenance, janitorial
Human resources	Labor relations Relocation Training Recruiting
Warehousing	Shipping Receiving Inventory, storage, and management
Cafeteria services	Cooking
Production	Assembly Packaging Processing
Building contractors	Power and lighting systems maintenance Electrical contracting
Nursing	On-call, fill-in positions

While the first three asterisked items were the most commonly mentioned during our interviews, there is likely to be an increase in the others as the benefits of non-core work become pronounced.

workforce should be treated as second class. Our interviewed leaders told us, loud and clear, that effective development of the external staff means ensuring they have close ties to the core.

MAKING THE NON-CORE WORKFORCE HUM

"What does it take for non-core staff members to succeed in your environment?" we asked. First and foremost was above-average competence in the job they are performing, i.e. their specialty skills. Peder Larson, President of Peder Larson Consulting LLC (former Commissioner of the Minnesota Pollution Control Agency), was very clear that while his core workforce is exceptionally talented because of its highly specialized abilities: "The technical expertise outside the agency has surpassed ours in quantity and, in many areas, in quality."

Next was a clear understanding of the organization the non-core staff are joining. This includes embracing values and beliefs similar to the host organization's, requiring external staff to be quick studies of organizational culture. They must read the informal, as well as the formal, rules of the road in each organization in which they work, then adapt accordingly.

Critical personal characteristics of the external non-core workforce, our interviewees said, are adaptability and flexibility in dealing with change and rapidly learning new skills. At Lawson Software, employees and business partners have access to the same classes which might even include clients. "Our challenge is to 'mindshare' with these partners," noted Mike Stringer.

Karl Stauber, of Northwest Area Foundation, described three interactive competencies necessary for non-core worker success. First, staff members must be self-starters, requiring low levels of supervision with a strong task-orientation and superb communication skills, especially the ability to ask good questions. Second, the organizational competencies must include a set of structures that treats all employees, core and non-core, equally and provides the support network they need. Third, the leader must display skills in hands-off management.

Leaders must begin now to develop a clear picture of the competencies they are looking for in their external workforce and initiate hiring practices that effectively identify those needed characteristics in prospective non-core staff. Many of our interviewees reported they are currently working with search firms that place non-core specialists, either individuals or small organizations, who can provide a given service. Box 2.5 delineates a list of key competencies desirable in the external workforce.

>> BOX 2.5 **Competencies of effective non-core staff**

- High-level specialty skills in the content of the job being performed.
- Ability to understand and embrace the host organization's culture by understanding its values, beliefs, and norms.
- Nimbleness in response to change.
- Capacity for quick learning.
- Understanding of the host organization's core business.
- Computer literacy (word processing, spread sheets, graphics).
- Creativity in work methodologies.
- Stellar team membership skills, including the ability to move in and out of teams adeptly.
- Self-management that includes planning, organizing, and executing work efficiently.

Interestingly, only the first competency (high-level specialty skills) emphasizes job content. The remainder focus on broad-brush knowledge and skills associated with organizational dimensions of learning, culture, change, and technology.

LEADERSHIP, 21ST-CENTURY STYLE

Lead with style and panache if you want to be successful in the 21st century. No more rigid, unimaginative, rule-bound, canned leadership approaches, our interviewees exclaimed! Most importantly, 21st-century leaders must possess communication capability so clear and concise, they can walk away and know the job will get done well. As Maggie Gagliardi, Senior Vice-President, Executive Resources and Staffing at American Express noted, the leader must have an "unshakable commitment to communication. We need to keep the communication channels open." Given the increasing number of staff working off-site, on-line, and around the globe, communication competencies will encompass more than face-to-face interactions. With technology as their primary medium, leaders must use these new tools in creative ways to drive home their messages – be it a change in corporate policy, a focus on the strategic direction, or day-to-day work management. They must make their presence known on-line, commanding attention without requiring frequent face-to-face contact.

Furthermore, effective leaders must be proficient in delegation and goal setting, coupled with the ability to trust good staff members to perform. This means staying out of their way. Herb Brandt, Vice-President of Employee Relations and Compliance at American Express pointed out: "You have to be able to truly delegate. Give them the authority to do the job because you're not there with them." Innovative leaders must build trusting relationships by focusing on deliverables, not just the numbers of hours staff members spend on the job. Letting go of traditional notions that staff have to be in a certain place, at a certain time in order to be working will be critical to leaders' abilities to manage in the new work arena. "Proximity should not be the critical variable of leadership," said Karl Stauber of Northwest Area Foundation.

Conducting an orchestra or juggling might be good hobbies for the 21st-century leader! Like a concert director orchestrating organizational components, leaders must assemble and reassemble them artfully, our interviewees stressed. Then, with many balls in the air at the same time, the leader must manage multiple people, projects, and locations simultaneously. Peter Gove, Vice-President of Corporate Relations at St Jude Medical, emphasized: "To manage a series of relationships at any given time, you cannot be only concrete sequential. You must draw on your intuitive skills." So, tomorrow's leaders must be quick-change artists, finding delight in spontaneity and serendipity – a break from the more linear, rational approaches so often associated with leadership best practices.

All the while, our interviewees said the 21st-century leader must worry about attracting and retaining good staff. Innovative incentive plans must align both financial and non-monetary rewards directly to performance. The leader must couple this with frequent inspiring communication that fosters "buy-in" to the mission, values, and goals – always keeping the "big picture" visible to every staff person. Leaders must study the people they want to lead, developing an in-depth understanding of an individual's unique needs. Mike Peterson, Senior Vice-President of Merchandise Planning and Merchandise Presentation at The Department Store Division of Dayton-Hudson Corporation (formerly Vice-President of Merchandise Planning for Target Stores), identified the need for leaders to be passionate, having an emotional connection to their work, totally absorbed and

> *Today's workforce wants to see excitement on the face of its leaders. They want to leave an encounter feeling inspired.*

committed. Today's workforce wants to see excitement on the face of its leaders. They want to leave an encounter feeling inspired. Box 2.6 provides a summary of 21st-century leadership competencies described by our interviewees.

➤➤ BOX 2.6   **Leadership competencies for the 21st century**

- Unshakable commitment to communication.
- Effective delegation by setting goals and trusting staff to deliver.
- Alignment of the workforce, core and non-core, to the organizational culture and mission.
- Assembly and reassembly of organizational components, including projects, teams, and locations.
- Multi-tasking while maintaining focus and continuity.
- Motivation across generational boundaries.
- Partnership-building.

Leadership competencies in the 21st century will be a juggling act between finite tasks and big-picture perspectives – all with the innovation of Disney and the co-ordination of a concert maestro.

NOT EVERYONE WANTS WHAT YOU WANT

Innovative leaders told us loud and clear that a keen awareness of generational differences is a critical factor in motivating their staff members, core and non-core, to high performance. For generation X (born from 1964 through 1975), growing up with computers and MTV (Music Television) and being the first generation of latchkey kids, it's no surprise that they are not used to being closely supervised. While loyal to a profession or a cause, they are not necessarily loyal to an organization, having witnessed the downsizing of many baby boomers. They are impatient and want rewards based on performance, not longevity or degrees, and don't understand why they should be required to work their way up if they have the necessary skills now (Bradford and Raines, 1992). As Xers enter the workforce, leaders of all generations will need to understand how best to lead and retain them because this is the thinnest labor pool in recent times. Specifically, the 35–44 year old age group will decline by 15 percent between the years 2000 and

2015 (Cliffe, 1998), a situation potentially placing further clamps on organizational productivity.

Baby boomers (born from 1946 through 1963) demonstrate strong work ethics and loyalty; they are typically willing to spend time talking through issues at length, scheduling many meetings, and engaging in face-to-face encounters as a means of getting work done. They have had good opportunities to build their careers and income base.

The oldest group working in organizations, the traditionalists (born from 1925 through 1945), value loyalty, respect for authority, and stability. Typically, they bring a strong work ethic, a wealth of life and work experiences, as well as commitment to the organizations fortunate enough to have captured their wisdom. And, while many traditionalists will move out of the workforce, still others will linger longer than ever before (Solomon, 1995).

Clearly, the same motivational strategies will not necessarily work for all segments of the workforce. "You must look at the boomers and Xers differently. Understand their skills and attributes," said Greg Hammill, formerly of AT&T, and now Chief Operating Officer for Talent Alliance.

NEW WAYS OF WORK PUT KNOWLEDGE MANAGEMENT IN THE SPOTLIGHT

The application of new technologies in the workplace is clearly driving the creation of new types of work and work titles, we learned from our interviewees (*see* Box 2.7). Knowledge work will take center stage. To understand what it is, consider the perspectives of Thomas Stewart, author of *Intellectual Capital: The New Wealth of Organizations*:

> *Intellectual capital is intellectual material – knowledge, information, intellectual property, experience – that can be put to use to create wealth. It is collective brainpower . . . In this new era, wealth is the product of knowledge. Knowledge and information – not just scientific knowledge, but news, advice, entertainment, communication, service – have become the economy's primary raw materials and its most important products. (Stewart, 1997, p. X)*

Knowledge work is the "brainpower" referred to by Stewart. While manual work in the US will continue its decline from 83 percent in 1900 to 41 percent by the year 2000, knowledge work will increase from 17 percent

>> BOX 2.7   **New types of work and work titles**

- Information-technology leaders – intranet/Internet managers, managers of electronic commerce, Web masters, and chief information or knowledge officers.

- Corporate relations/communication managers – leaders of internal and external communication around corporate strategy, image, and reputation.

- Internal consultants – specialists with fine-tuned expertise.

- Team leaders/project leaders – coordinators of individuals and assignments, usually from a cross-functional perspective.

- Universal counselors – handlers of every aspect of a function; this becomes their "specialization."

- Managers of non-core workforce – leaders who bring non-core staff into the organization and facilitate their integration.

- Global specialists – experts in foreign languages and culture.

All these roles are associated with the explosion of knowledge work in organizations.

to 59 percent during this same period (Stewart, 1997). We'll still need people to build office towers, deliver packages, and lay underground pipes, but more jobs will involve knowledge work than has occurred in history.

"Knowledge gurus," as Life USA Holding, Inc. calls them, will be pivotal to steering organizations through the maze of relentless information explosions. Knowledge managers of all types will manage the flow of information within the organization and from outside in, helping staff members screen what is applicable to their work at any given time. They may play several of the following roles:

- technology expert: understands available technology and cheerleads its use to its fullest potential;

- cataloger/archivist: organizes information for practical use;

- guide: directs individuals to outside sources of information;

- scout: sorts out critical information useful for the organization and manages the information flow;

- research librarian: prioritizes relevant information and assists users in defining information needs;

- analyst: creates a context for understanding information and considers patterns for new areas of interest;

- debriefer: identifies internal best practices (Williams and Bukowitz, 1997).

Robert Stevens, President and CEO of Ridgeview Medical Center in Waconia, Minnesota, told us: "The differentiating point [between organizations] is how you analyze and interpret information. Information is often not analyzed for you ... [you must] tailor the information to the individual and the organization." Knowledge management will be crucial to organizational survival, said our interviewees.

Knowledge moves on a continuum from specialist to generalist. While we've been talking about specialized knowledge, there is emerging a new type of knowledge professional that some call "universal counselors" who handle every aspect of a given function. Robin Zelkowitz, Vice-President of Employee Relations and Compliance for American Express, explained: "In the past, people focused on a specific function or customer. Now, you take care of every function. You handle whatever the problem is." This generalist role, ironically, is becoming a new type of specialty.

Other new types of work emanating in our interviewees' organizations include internal consultation roles. Human resource and information systems functions were noted to be rapidly repositioning themselves with a focus on providing consultative services to their internal customers, often competing with outside vendors to maintain their functions internally. This requires they operate as nearly independent business units, growing their market share of available work within their companies, and sometimes, contracting out their services to other organizations.

Much of the new work will be project work that comes and goes, dramatically reducing the usefulness of formal job descriptions. Project teams will be assembled and disbanded as quickly as projects are developed and completed. With this flow will come the blurring of lines between team leader and member. In any one project, the team leader role will really be a facilitator of the process, perhaps on a rotating basis. The team leader one month may become a team member the next, and vice versa. Projects will be cross-functional with representation from a number of areas and may include non-core and core staff. Adding yet another dimension, team members are likely to be geographically dispersed, working through technology as the primary communication mode. Knowledge professionals will gain recognition and status, making them desirable team members or leaders, by the wealth of information they store-house as well as by their ability to access and interpret information astutely. And knowledge leaders will be needed to manage the flow of knowledge. This is more pronounced than most realize: "More than 40 percent of Fortune 1000 companies have named knowledge officers or put knowledge management programs in place" (Leonard, 1997, p. A18).

THE WORKPLACE IN THE FUTURE TENSE: A WHOLE NEW LOOK

Our interviewees confirmed that more work will be done at a variety of locations – home, remote office locations, and at customer sites. A focus on buildings as the primary place for doing work is fast being replaced by on-line environments. The virtual workplace will soon be the norm, allowing people to work on their own schedules, breaking down the notion that everyone must come to a workplace at about the same time each day.

President and Chief Operating Officer Maggie Hughes of Life USA Holding, Inc., though, put up a red flag related to technological development. She told us a marriage between technology and personal business relationships is crucial. Technology should be used to enhance personal contact, not replace it, and therefore she is leading her organization into new technologies carefully, with an eye on their real usefulness in building better customer service.

Box 2.8 profiles the workscape of the future being created now by our interviewees.

►► BOX 2.8 **Profile of the workscape of the future**

- Technology is the primary communication vehicle through which work is done.
- Virtual workspaces are as common as the morning commute is now.
- Office space moves beyond "cubicles" to more mobile, migrating work station components.
- Fluid organizational structures replace chain-of-command, segmented, and functional models, blurring traditional boundaries.
- Job security results from staff members' proven track records, being known as really good at something the organization or profession values.

LEARNING À LA CARTE: CUSTOMIZED OPTIONS

As the need for immediate, just-in-time training swells, our interviewees described their organizations' development of technology-based training, including the use of intra- and Internet Web sites as well as satellite dishes placed at customer sites for product education. The key theme was immediacy – the need to get information to the workforce and customers quickly.

Curt Hilliker, Facility and Services Director of Andersen Consulting, Boston office, told us his organization is moving toward individualized training. A Professional Development Plan (PDP), which lays out all the skills a staff person may need or want, is created at Andersen Consulting with prescribed time lines for completion of training activities. Interactive computer training is provided to allow individuals to complete their PDP at times most convenient for them and to avoid having to wait for a class to be available. The product applications are so intuitive, however, users can go beyond just learning how to use them to actually creating value with them. For example, executives need minimal training in how to navigate a financial software package that is nearly self-explanatory. Instead, the training focus is on how to create value with the tool.

Through joint ventures with higher education institutions, some interviewees noted virtual universities are being established. This might entail selecting the best courses from a variety of universities and packaging them, through a broker-like organization, in order to meet specific needs. At the University of St Thomas in Minneapolis, the MBA Program in Medical Group Management consists of classes conducted via the Internet; students need only to come to campus two weeks a year for "live" classroom interaction. Class discussions, simulations, and small-group exercises are all conducted over the Net. This is particularly advantageous for working adult students who, in this program, are nurses, physicians, medical technologists, and healthcare managers. According to Tom Gilliam, Director of this innovative program:

> *When potential students consider our program, it's a matter of choosing the right delivery modality to meet their learning and lifestyle needs. Programs like this need to consider delivering the right product to the right audience in the right way at the right time.*

It was clear as we spoke with our leaders that training, more and more, would have to be clearly linked to the organizational vision and mission. Just providing interesting classes with no bottom-line value will not be adequate in the 21st century. Furthermore, competency testing is considered to be more crucial than ever to provide evidence that training programs lead to skill development. This is critical as knowledge work becomes more complex. It has been predicted that by the year 2010, "it will take 50 percent of a work day to come up to speed with what's transpired since you left the day before" (McGuire, 1998, p. 10).

Box 2.9 gives a summary of what innovative leaders are working on now to bring their training practices into the 21st century.

➤➤ BOX 2.9 **Design and delivery of learning**

- Immediate learning, on call as needed or wanted:
  - delivered through corporate intranet or the Internet
  - continuously updated content
  - self-paced.
- Content developed internally or with partner:
  - virtual universities providing the best available instruction on a given topic
  - vendors with specialized expertise designing training.
- Learning closely aligned with the organization's vision, mission, and goals – content screened carefully and continually for relevancy.
- Assurance that learning has occurred – competency testing becomes more prevalent.

Here's what leaders will need to do to bring training practices into the 21st century.

WORDS OF WISDOM

In summary, we asked for advice from the leaders we interviewed. What would they share with other leaders regarding how to prepare for the future? What behaviors won't work in a changing work environment? They offered many wise words: listen to and empower others during organizational change; have your ear to the ground and draw out ideas to ensure staff members have a true voice, thereby creating commitment; don't deny the discomfort change brings, but deal with it by acknowledging, supporting, and discussing the stressors.

Develop flexibility and adaptability in your own behavior and mindset, our leaders said. This first comes about by reading, studying, and staying up to date. Maggie Hughes of Life USA Holding, Inc., said, "I don't care what you read. Read three to four books each month." Greg Hammill of Talent Alliance emphasized the importance of modeling flexibility when he said, "Be willing to try new things yourself first. Others must see you, the leader, changing your behavior, setting the standard."

Never underestimate human needs and strive to fulfill them. The 21st-century leader must understand what drives individuals to want to succeed. Position power is a thing of the past and will become even more unimportant. You must lead people in a direction rather than tell them where to go. Create images of a compelling future and move people down that path through inspiring, consistent, and persuasive communication.

> *Create images of a compelling future and move people down that path through inspiring, consistent, and persuasive communication.*

Stop patronizing the workforce. Don't assume you know what they need; rather, work closely with them and discuss their needs and career aspirations. Genuinely believe that any individual is worthy of your time. Look at each individual, identifying their unique drives. Respect the differences among the generations and strive to build a work environment sensitive to the values they espouse.

Pinpoint your organization's core competencies, then perform them better than anyone else. Don't spread yourself too thin, yet think about a global playing field. Focus. Box 2.10 summarizes advice from innovative leaders.

STOP DOING THESE THINGS – NOW

We asked our interviewees what leadership behaviors should be thrown away, i.e. what simply won't work in the 21st century given the new landscape they've described. Most importantly, they said, stop focusing on the immediate day-to-day tasks and begin to thing more long-term, putting strategies into place now that position the organization for the future. Think about opportunity all the time.

Stop thinking segmentally, as if the area you lead is an autonomous business unit. Instead, think integration, both in the marketplace and in your own organization, searching for collaborative partnerships. Replace

---

>> BOX 2.10 **Advice from innovative leaders**

- Always remain up to date with very current information.
- Develop adaptability and flexibility in yourself and your organization.
- Listen to staff at all levels of your organization and distribute power throughout change.
- Strive to understand and fulfill the human needs of your workforce and customers.
- Keep a global focus.
- Run yourself and the unit you lead like a business.
- Learn not to be arrogant; believe others are worthy of your time.
- Understand that position power is unimportant.
- Communicate clearly and passionately about the direction of your organization.
- Manage expectations about technology; it can't do everything.
- Find out what is not working in the organization and address it.
- Recognize and capitalize upon your workforce's diversity in skill sets and career paths.

---

silos with webs of interconnected relationships spun around capturing business opportunities.

Stop behaving like a "boss" and discard any tendencies toward arrogance you may have. Avoid being condescending to, and overprotective of, your workforce. "Change your leadership style in the direction of trust, rather than control," Gerhard Bihl of BMW advised. Resist the urge to think others want what you want from their work. Different generations and workforce segments require different motivational strategies.

Discard any notion you may have that your staff must be permanent and full-time. Open the doors to new work arrangements which include performance contracts for non-core staff in many different configurations – a just-in-time workforce. Shift your notion of work from jobs having rigid boundaries to work assignments having greater amounts of integration between and among organization units, with less structured parameters. "Dejob" (Bridges, 1994) your thinking patterns as well as your work environment.

Stop being impatient; rather, give things some time to work without over-reacting. Learn from "failure" and openly share the learning. Stop thinking everything has to be done correctly the first time it's attempted.

Become more experimental. While teams will remain dominant and productive components of organizational design, allow room for individual creativity to emerge. Create space for mavericks; don't let teams consume individual spirit.

IT'S NOW OR NEVER

As you've just learned, there is no time to waste. Innovative leaders who have the long view are not sitting back to see what the future will bring. They are exchanging old thinking patterns and behaviors for new ones – they are doing *Fast Forward Leadership*.

If you are going to be a leader you must also make change now. If you wait much longer, your chance of being able to catch up is hampered. The risks of being sluggish are great, both to your personal career survival and to the workforce who rely on your wisdom.

> *The risks of being sluggish are great, both to your personal career survival and to the workforce who rely on your wisdom.*

Chart your course using the strategies we've laid out in the chapters ahead. We'll show you exactly what to do now to join the ranks of innovative leaders yourself.

REFERENCES

Bradford, L. J. and Raines, C. (1992) *Twentysomething: Managing and Motivating Today's New Workforce*. New York: MasterMedia.

Bridges, W. (1994) *JobShift: How to Prosper in a Workplace Without Jobs*. Reading, Massachusetts: Addison-Wesley Publishing Company.

Cliffe, S. (1998) "Winning the war for talent," *Harvard Business Review*, 76 (5), 18–19.

Leonard, M. (1997) "The business of knowledge," *Star Tribune*, 26 June.

McGuire, P. A. (1998) "Wanted: Workers with flexibility for 21st century jobs," *Monitor*, July. Washington, DC: American Psychological Association.

Solomon, C. (1995). "Unlock the potential of older workers," *Personnel Journal*, 74 (10), 56–66.

Stewart, T. A. (1997) *Intellectual Capital: The New Wealth of Organizations*. New York: Doubleday/Currency.

Williams, R. L. and Bukowitz, W. R. (1997) "Knowledge managers guide information seekers," *HRMagazine*, 42 (1), 76–81.

THE COMMUNICATION EXCHANGE

Limited and informational for shared and persuasive

P|atrick MacDonald is a mid-career manager who oversees the production of one of his company's product lines, packaging for disk drives. He has been working there for over 15 years and has a reputation as a good leader, particularly in his ability to apply effective technical solutions to problems the product line has encountered. Patrick has 32 staff members organized into four packaging teams that report directly to him and he is part of several cross-functional groups that oversee quality, product support, and new product development. This group includes staff members at remote locations. Several significant changes are brewing within the company which Patrick must communicate to his staff. In addition, his packaging teams have generated a number of interesting new product ideas he would like others in the company to consider.

Patrick is in his office today preparing a memo to circulate to his staff informing them of the upcoming changes the company is proposing. His outline includes what the change is, the reason for the change, the time line for implementation, and a call for cooperation from the staff members. Next, he turns his attention to communicating his staff members' suggestions to others who are members of the cross-functional group he leads. He writes a fax with a bulleted list of their ideas, asking for feedback. Next, he gives the rough drafts, typed via the two-finger method on his PC, to his assistant to polish-up and send. Then, he dashes off a few additional faxes and memos with announcements. He looks through his e-mail – over 150 – and responds to the most urgent ones, saving the others for a later time, annoyed that the volume seems to be growing exponentially. "Now that my communication is complete," says Patrick to himself, "I can get back to working through the technical snag we've uncovered on one of the packaging lines."

Frankly, Patrick is communicating like a dinosaur. Surrounding him in his workspace is a set of technical tools – e-mail, groupware, and videoconferencing – he has not yet mastered or utilizes minimally. The content of his memo on corporate changes lacks inspiration and most likely will not gain the staff support he needs to drive implementation. His choice of communication vehicle – a memo – is hardly an appropriate way to introduce significant change. Patrick has fallen into several communication traps. He should stop these behaviors now. Here's why.

COMMUNICATION TRAPS TO SIDE-STEP

As we've worked with a wide variety of organizations in our consulting practices, we are often struck by their seemingly inadequate communication strategies as new technologies have been introduced. As the volume of interchange has grown, the control has not always been put in place, resulting in massive communication overload. It is not uncommon for staff members, for example, with e-mail capability to receive as many as 200 messages each day. Ouch! Keeping on top of that volume can be overwhelming and painful.

And, as the MTV generation (*see* Chapter 5 for more details) has come on the work scene, many leaders seemingly have neglected the need to develop a more inspirational, passionate, and, even, entertaining communication style. Their communiqué seems dull, at times, uninspired and unlikely to stand out among the barrage of messages staff members are buried under. One of the most striking examples of this can be found by reading most organizational mission statements which drone on something like this: "Our mission is to serve our customers by providing good products and/or services." Inspirational? Motivating? Exciting? Passionate? We don't think so.

To begin to transform your communication approach, stop doing these things now, if these behaviors have slipped into your communication style. Here is "The communication exchange: limited and informational for shared and persuasive."

STOP DOING THESE THINGS

1 Stop informing rather than persuading

With change being the norm rather than the exception in most organizations today, leaders must stop thinking of communication as an exercise in information dissemination alone. The workforce today, particularly the younger portion, consistently requests more "why" and less "what." Consider for a moment how much of the communication you initiate is in the form of briefing sessions, FYIs, and announcements. How much of it gives adequate explanation of the reasons for what you describe is happening?

2 Stop ignoring technological tools or using them incorrectly

We often are asked by our generation X (*see* Chapter 5) seminar participants why their managers are so reluctant or inept at utilizing the technology available to them. Having grown up with computers as a primary means of communication, these younger staff members are puzzled by their leaders and co-workers who insist on countless face-to-face meetings when, in their opinion, an on-line conversation would suffice. They nearly chuckle at the attachment to fax and "snail mail" these colleagues seem to have. They seem annoyed by the lack of technological savvy displayed in the communication they do receive.

The biggest obstacle to increased use of technological work tools has been the manager's discomfort (Hequet, 1994). Since the bulk of today's managers are baby boomers and traditionalists, we suspect they are simply uncomfortable with a communication method they did not grow up with or use extensively in their early careers. And, some have not stayed current with technological developments and are unfamiliar with these new communication tools. Does unfamiliarity breed contempt? We hope not. Leaders of the 21st century will need to break through this barrier and accept the virtual and mobile workplace as their playing field, navigating it with skill and ease. This will require abandoning the notion that good leadership requires constant face-to-face communication. Greg Hammill of Talent Alliance predicts baby-boomer managers will combine virtual office technologies with face-to-face communication. As these managers begin to exit the workforce, the generation Xers who assume leadership roles will create more full-fledged virtual organizations. Are we sure we want to wait that long?

Leaders need to stop underutilizing the technology sitting at their fingertips. By not becoming adept at cyberspace navigation, you may run the risk of losing credibility with those more adroit than you.

> *Leaders need to stop underutilizing the technology sitting at their fingertips.*

Even more importantly, productivity and efficiency may suffer in an era when speed is of the essence.

3 Stop undermanaging communication content and dissemination

The advent of more technological tools has created an abundance of unmanaged communication. It's just too tempting to forward copies of every e-mail and voice mail you receive when a push of a button makes it so simple. In the absence of communication guidelines, the volume can easily become out of control, burying staff members in more communication than they can possibly manage.

No longer does information move up and down the ladder of the hierarchy, but, rather, moves here, there, and everywhere. Access to information has opened up like flood gates and organizations need to develop ways to ensure the information is being utilized effectively. As the workforce becomes more involved in decision making, we believe it is critical that staff members have access to information formerly available only to managers. However, they must know how to access and use the information to make informed decisions.

Technology adds more options to the modes we can use to communicate and, therefore, presents great opportunity for organizations to go into information overload. As a leader, it is essential that you stop allowing this phenomenon to spread throughout your organization like an infectious disease.

4 Stop undercommunicating the most important stuff

John Kotter's (1995) research at Harvard University indicates that leaders communicate ten times less than they should when leading significant organizational change. Consequently, the rumor mill becomes overactive as staff members scramble to share what information they have heard. Too little shared information can be misleading, producing paranoia and undue stress, damaging productivity and morale.

Undercommunication can also mean too little listening. Leaders sometimes forget that communication has two parts: sending and receiving.

5 Stop faking it

Unfortunately, in our opinions, too many leaders pretend to listen to their staff. They ask for ideas and input, then don't follow up. The upshot is a disheartened team, feeling powerless and manipulated. Leaders may develop a great big credibility gap, losing their staff's trust. Don't risk it.

6 Stop thinking locally

Leaders of today should consider the globe as their playing field. Your staff may now, or in the future, work worldwide, in person and/or on-line. Therefore, cross-cultural understanding becomes a prerequisite to effective cross-cultural communication. Thinking locally will not prepare you or your staff to meet this challenge, so stop limiting your scope.

To avoid the communication traps we've just identified, start to do the following things to update and build your communication know-how. These "starts" focus on two key aspects of communication: the content and the form.

START DOING THESE THINGS

1 Start thinking of yourself as a salesperson

Think of every communication you send as a presentation. It must be well-oiled, polished, and add meaning to data. It must do more than inform: it must persuade, interpret, and educate (Lindstrom, 1998).

In the past, staff members worked with groups of people for long periods of time and developed a shared body of knowledge and experiences. Now, with virtual teams becoming more the norm, staff must work quickly and be very good at what they do. Leaders have to communicate values and purpose, not just ideas to help staff – who may be spread all over the world – internalize the bigger meaning of their work. John Seely Brown, chief scientist at Xerox Corporation, who is known for his work in communication and learning processes, says the key communication skill in the digital age will be the art of storytelling. He believes image literacy will be as important as textual literacy. Communication will truly be an artform (Lindstrom, 1998).

> *Persuasion begins with a careful analysis of your audience. Put yourself in their shoes and gear the message to them.*

Persuasion begins with a careful analysis of your audience. Put yourself in their shoes and gear the message to them. The fundamental element of persuasive communication lies in answering these questions: "What's in it for your audience to buy-in to your idea; utilize the information you're sending; commit to this change?" In other words, "Why should they care?" Box 3.1 provides a template for persuasive communication.

➤➤ BOX 3.1 **Template for persuasive communication**

1 Analyze the audience

- What do you want them to do as a result of your communication?
- What do they need to know in order to understand your message?
- What are the expected benefits to them?
- What are the expected disadvantages to them?

2 Outline your message

- Introduce the topic. Give background information to help the audience understand the need for what you are proposing.
  - Use stories, anecdotes, startling statistics to grab attention and create an emotional response.
  - Indicate what's wrong with the way things are now, when introducing change. Sell the need. What problem will this change solve?
- State the idea, clearly and succinctly. Think sound-bite.
  - Delineate supporting evidence. Make sure it is well-documented and researched.
  - Decide which facts are most critical. Don't overload.
  - State the key ideas using metaphors or vivid words.
- Close with a call to action.
  - What do you want others to do?
  - What will happen next?

3 Choose the best communication channel: which is most likely to capture your audience?

Find your passion and speak from the heart. The best leaders we know develop their "stump" speech – the most important things they want their staff to do – then, repeat the message "every day in every way." Consequently, the message is delivered continually, not occasionally. What's most important for leaders to drive home are the overarching principles, values, and strategic goals: "Customers are our first priority," "Quality cannot be sacrificed," "Think outside the box – innovate." Maggie Hughes of Life USA Holding, Inc. does this particularly well, not surprisingly, given her background as a former communication consultant. She continually emphasizes the need for owners (the term used for staff members, all of whom are required to own stock) to understand the business, and utilizes both formal and informal communication to teach business strategy. In a recent owners' forum, which she conducts routinely, Maggie was asked by an owner if it was realistic to be introducing a new product on such an ambitious time line. She challenged the owner to rethink the question, explaining the company's core business was innovative product development and without new products it would not succeed. She suggested the owner ask, "How can we get this product out the door by the end of the year? What will it take and how can I make it happen?"

Larkin and Larkin (1994) found that communication about comparative performance of a work unit or company was the best persuasive tactic to generate change. When regions looked at their performance compared to other regions, when work methods were benchmarked against best practices in the field, or when comparative financial performance data show a clear decline, staff tend to take heed.

2 Start cranking up your technosmarts

Complete the checklist in Box 3.2 to determine your level of basic technological savvy. Begin at once to develop skills in those areas you discovered you may not be proficient.

Next, learn to choose the right tool for the communication job at hand. The menu is before you. Will it be voice mail, e-mail, videoconferencing, face-to-face meeting, memo, fax, or a combo? Here are some guidelines to help you make the right choice.

>> BOX 3.2 **Basic technological savvy checklist**

I have keyboard skills or voice-activated e-mail capability. ❏

I can utilize all major functions available in my e-mail system. ❏

I can utilize all major functions in my word-processing program. ❏

I can utilize all major functions in my spreadsheet program. ❏

I utilize presentations graphics software (e.g. PowerPoint) for visual aids when speaking before a group. ❏

I can proficiently utilize the Internet and my organization's intranet to search for information. ❏

I can proficiently utilize all major databases (e.g. financial, materials management, customer tracking) that are relevant to my work. ❏

I am proficient in setting up an audioconference. ❏

I am proficient in setting up a videoconference. ❏

I can utilize all the major functions on my voice-mail system. ❏

I carry a laptop, or variation of a Palm Pilot, and utilize all its major functions, including e-mail, when traveling. ❏

I regularly update my technological skills and knowledge via training, reading, and interaction with technology professionals. ❏

Begin at once to master the competencies listed here that you did not check off and are most relevant to your work.

Electronic mail

For quick information exchange, this is the mode to choose. E-mail allows us to communicate globally with ease, given all parties have access to the technology. Beware. E-mail is not a good choice when sensitive, confidential messages must be sent. Even though you delete from your on-line file cabinet a message that you have sent, it remains in the hard drive of your organization's computer system. It may come back to haunt you, particularly if you become involved in a lawsuit.

A perfect example is dramatized in the training video, "Avoiding Litigation Land Mines" produced by the Kenwood Group of Coastal Human Resources, Virginia. A manager is shown communicating about a problem staff member she was intending to fire. In a moment of frustration, she darts off an e-mail to a colleague saying the employee is "like an old man driving 40 in the fast lane." The e-mail, which had been archived on the company's hard drive, was produced in court when the employee sued for wrongful termination. Box 3.3 summarizes e-mail etiquette to keep you and your staff from this embarrassing and costly situation.

Telephone and voice mail

When you need to hear someone's voice tone and handle somewhat fragile situations at a time when face-to-face communication is not feasible, the telephone should be your communication mode of choice. Telephone conversations do provide confidentiality and the free exchange of dialogue.

Voice mail is a bit more complicated. While a valuable tool for communicating information when you can't reach someone personally, it provides no assurances the message was received and/or interpreted accurately. Since voice mail can be broadcast, it can be an effective way to get a more personalized message to a large group, even the whole organization. Beware. Voice mail, like e-mail, is not confidential. Any message you send can be forwarded on to others, so make sure your voice mail is fit for distribution.

Use your telephone system to communicate with some imagination. Two-way telephone lines can carry information – company news, product updates, answers to frequently asked questions – to be accessed from any place a staff person or customer might be.

Fax

Fax is a good mode for communicating printed information when e-mail is not accessible to all and wide distribution is the aim. Or, when a document cannot be scanned into e-mail, fax may be the best alternative. A broadcast fax, for example, can get information to remote sites quickly and completely. Remember, again, that fax is a one-way communication mode so you cannot manage the information interpretation or ensure it was received.

Meetings

It's been estimated that 11 million meetings are convened each day in the United States, amounting to 100 million hours of professional and executive productivity. Additionally, a 3M survey of visitors to their Web site (www.3m.com/meetings) found that meetings are more frequent than ever before, most likely because of the increase in participatory decision making

▶▶ BOX 3.3 E-mail etiquette

When sending an e-mail message

- Use the subject line to indicate key information, assuming the receiver may be scanning multiple message lines.

- Don't attach large files without approval from the recipient; they can be difficult to download.

- Assume the message is permanent; don't send anything confidential or personal.

- Choose your recipients carefully; don't overload people with information they don't need.

- Use a conversational but courteous tone. Recognize that all capital letters means you're screaming!

- Clearly indicate when you are expressing your opinion and when you are sharing facts.

- Do not rant or use offensive language.

- Get to the point. Limiting your message to one screen of text is a good rule of thumb.

- Use e-mail to foster connections, not to avoid face-to-face encounters.

- Use e-mail creatively; for instance, to offer feedback, to brainstorm electronically, and to give brief, on-line training sessions.

- Use emoticons to add expression to your e-mail. :-) means "get it?" or "just joking!", ;) is a wink, :- (expresses sadness or disappointment, g> is a grin.

- When posting to a discussion group, stay on the topic. Others may see it as rude to introduce something already discussed or off-topic dialogue. If the group has a list of frequently asked questions, consult it before entering the dialogue.

When receiving e-mail messages

- Respond with the "reply" button to ensure all addresses are automatically included with the return message.

- Promptly forward messages intended for others.

- Promptly respond to messages – within 24–48 hours. (But if a message makes you angry or upset, give yourself time to relax and reflect before answering.)

- Watch out for unsolicited attachments. Don't download them because they may include a virus.

- Don't interrupt your work whenever a message arrives.

Source: Adapted from Hartman and Nantz, 1995, Cohen, 1996, and Sabath, 1998

and teamwork. Secondly, they found meetings are more interactive, focusing on group problem solving and decision making. Last, they discovered meetings often involve one or more remote participants (Hanke, 1998).

These trends give today's leader a strong message: fully incorporate technology into your meeting venues. Teleconferencing, audioconferencing, videoconferencing, and dataconferencing via group decision-support software (discussed in the "team exchange," Chapter 6) all provide ways for leaders to meet with their staff without the time and expense of travel.

Teleconferencing allows participants to meet via telephone. When multiple staff members are at one site, typically they huddle around a speaker phone to converse with those at other sites. Often wrought with echoing and static, teleconferencing still saves time and expense. Audioconferencing technology reduces echoes and delays, producing better sound as long as each participant or site has units installed (Dixon, 1998). Box 3.4 gives guidelines for teleconferencing and audioconferencing.

➤➤ BOX 3.4   **Guidelines for teleconferencing and audioconferencing**

Preparation
- Make sure the purpose of the meeting is clear.
- Distribute an agenda and supporting materials.
- Familiarize yourself with your organization's teleconferencing technology or arrange to use outside services.
- Distribute some teleconferencing tips, if participants are inexperienced:
  - identify yourself before speaking;
  - if multiple staff members are at one site, don't talk only to one another.

During
- Start on time.
- Review the agenda.
- Solicit opinions from everyone.
- Assign a recorder.
- Thank everyone for their participation.

After
- Make sure minutes are sent out.
- Follow up on action items.

Videoconferencing adds the ability to see participants, and, therefore opens another important level of communication – the ability to observe non-verbal information. When relationship building is of the essence and the topics are complex, this mode will serve you best. The cost of videoconferencing has plummeted recently while the technical quality of transmission has increased, suggesting videoconferencing is about to go mainstream.

Videoconferencing capability can mean far more than just meeting. Healthcare organizations have rapidly moved into telemedicine as a way of consulting on patient diagnosis and treatment. Mayo Clinic in Rochester, Minnesota is seen as leader in this field, having utilized the technology since 1993. Their network brings together the Scottsdale and Jacksonville clinics with the Rochester site. Desktop video is scheduled next, projected to be in place by 1999 (Lindstrom, 1998). Box 3.5 provides tips on how to hold productive videoconferences.

Are face-to-face meetings obsolete? We don't think so; just overused for the wrong purpose. Too often leaders hold meetings to disseminate information with minimal participant interaction – not a good idea, given the communication alternatives we've discussed. Face-to-face meetings do build relationships, and continue to provide the best forum for discussing difficult issues. When communicating organizational change, Larkin and Larkin (1994) found there was no substitute for face-to-face communication if the leader's objective is to build commitment.

No matter what communication channels your organization utilizes, one thing is clear. Make sure all staff members are trained in how both to lead and participate effectively in meetings. The biggest complaints we hear about meetings in any form are that they are poorly prepared, lack good facilitation, and don't include the right people. No meeting, no matter what mode of interaction is utilized, will be successful unless the staff involved have sharpened their meeting skills.

3 Start setting communication standards

Don't let communication overload dominate your organization. Insist that work units employ rules concerning what gets communicated to whom, how often, and by whom. Once overload sets in, staff members begin to ignore a substantial amount of the communication they receive. Sometimes, leaders forget that all

> *Insist that work units employ rules concerning what gets communicated to whom, how often, and by whom.*

> **►► BOX 3.5** **Guidelines for videoconferencing**

1 Arrange the conference and determine equipment needs at the base site and remote sites.

2 Prepare. Prepare. Prepare.
- Make sure graphics are extra clear and legible.
- Distribute materials.
- Choose a chairperson for each remote site to organize discussions.

3 Dress properly.
- Avoid plaids, prints, and stripes, which appear to move on screen.
- Avoid white and red, which make you appear washed out.
- Choose medium shades or pastels.

4 Learn how to work the equipment.
- Place visuals where they can be seen by the camera.
- Rehearse with the conference control panel.

5 Use effective presentation methods.
- Let your personality come through.
- Identify yourself and others if you're working with multiple sites.
- Pause as you finish each comment to allow for a slight delay in reception images.
- Avoid making loud noises the microphone might pick up.
- Announce that you are showing graphics.

6 Run the meeting effectively.
- Begin with a roll-call of each location and introduce participants.
- Review the agenda.
- Be aware of which camera you're using. Switch smoothly from the main camera to the graphics camera. Vary your camera use from the zoom to wide-angle to add variety.
- End by reviewing assignments.

Source: Adapted from "Tangible benefits of videoconferencing", *The New Way to Office*. Kinko's, 1 (2)

parts of the organization may not be fully "wired" and, therefore, lose access to some communication. With flattening organization structures and more cross-functional team approaches, it is not always clear to whom staff members should go to get information. Therefore, guidelines must be installed as suggested in Box 3.6.

> ➤➤ BOX 3.6

Guidelines required for managing organizational communication

- What constitutes an urgent communication.
- Who needs copies and forwards of what kinds of information.
- What information should go to whom.
- Frequency with which files, electronic and otherwise, should be purged.
- Expected response time for each type of communication.
- Expected length of communication (typical standard includes one screen maximum for e-mail, one page maximum for memos and letters).
- Meeting norms (e.g. start and end on time, come prepared, limit routine meetings to one hour, use respectful communication).

4 Start getting buy-in through real participation and ownership

Communicating persuasively and listening actively are only part of the formula for effective communication. Interaction – live or via technology – is the critical variable in what we believe a potent leader must demonstrate. By ensuring staff are actively involved in decisions that affect them, leaders will maximize the brain power running rampant in their organizations. We've devised the continuum of decision-making options (Fig. 3.1) to help you cultivate staff participation.

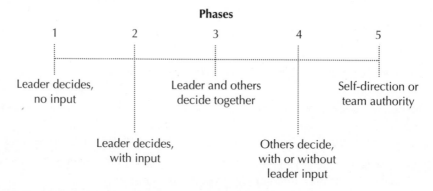

Fig 3.1 ■ Continuum of decision-making options

Here's how it works. A leader should systematically and thoughtfully propel staff to move from left (no participation) to right (self- or team authority) on the continuum, releasing control as they demonstrate more commitment and ability. Rothwell (1996) indicates that lower levels of participation yield decreased benefits in two ways – decreased organizational effectiveness and employee job satisfaction.

Phase 1: leader decides, no input

The continuum begins on the left with the first phase. The leader makes a decision without input from others. In our work, we have discovered the best situations for applying this style include times of crisis, when the individual/team does not have the requisite skills to contribute to the decision, or when the individual or team may not care about the decision or be affected by it. Leaders must do a diligent job of explaining why they are making the decision primarily alone and the forms of support they will need from those who will implement it.

Phase 2: leader decides, with input

The decision is clearly the leader's here, but the leader directly solicits feedback and has a responsibility to inform others how it was utilized to make the decision. Set the ground rules up front: you want the input, will consider it, but may not use all of it. Then, complete the loop; report back on what input you did use and how, as well as why you rejected some of what you heard. If you really have no intention of reflecting on the input, then go back to phase 1 on the continuum. Messages that do not match your actions create more harm than good.

Phase 3: leader and others decide together

In the third phase of the continuum the leader becomes part of the decision-making group. Here, your voice is simply one of many; the rule of decision making is consensus – discussing until a group mindset is reached on the issue. We recommend voting only as a last resort because it may divide the group into "winners" and "losers." Researchers and practitioners of change management corroborate that involvement in decision making may lead to higher-quality decisions and higher commitment to the final outcome (Nevis, Lancourt, and Vassallo, 1996). When utilizing this phase of the continuum, a leader must facilitate, drawing ideas from others and guiding, not dominating, decision-making processes.

Phase 4: others decide, with or without leader input

When using the fourth phase of the model, the leader literally gets out of the way, allowing others to make decisions independently. The leader serves as a resource to the individual or group, on-call as needed. He or she still needs to set the goal, provide parameters, and even re-direct if needed. The leader's role is to delegate, get out of way, but not disappear. From the sidelines, s/he must be available to coach, give feedback, and troubleshoot.

Phase 5: self-direction or team authority

Leaders using this phase would engage individuals or teams to become autonomous – managing their own functions, projects, and activities. Here, the team may decide their own leadership method, compensation system, work tasks, and performance management. The leader becomes the champion, heralding the entire team's efforts to the rest of the organization while remaining uninvolved in the bulk of day-to-day decisions. Advocacy and coaching is the leader's role at this phase.

5 Start listening more

Another critical way to gain staff commitment and boost morale is to focus not only on sending messages, but on receiving information. Many staff members don't believe their leaders understand their concerns. Here's a test. Can you list the top five concerns of your staff members, right now, without making any telephone calls? If not, begin to boost your listening behavior immediately, or you may soon be a victim of leader isolation, cut off from critical information from which others protect you. As leaders become more removed from the informal communication networks, or if they do not invite critical feedback, they will find the information that flows to them through formal channels is likely to be sanitized. No one really wants to be the bearer of bad news, unless the leader rewards the critic by listening, responding, then taking action.

A leader can listen in a variety of ways. Norm Brown, the new CEO of Partners of the Americas, an international organization of volunteers in both North and South America, is beginning his tenure by traveling to each region of the Unites States and Latin America to conduct "listening sessions," asking volunteers what their needs are. Other organizational leaders routinely conduct extensive audits of their staff members which include personal interviews, group meetings, and written surveys. The data are then used to make change. Starbucks, the Seattle-based coffee company, conducts an on-line suggestion and idea program and staff members are encouraged to e-mail ideas to their managers (Vander Houwen, 1997). Listening can occur via technology, remember, as well as face-to-face.

6 Start thinking globally

For those staff members who work across cultures, make sure they have adequate training in cross-cultural communication. While English is the most-studied language throughout the world, that doesn't guarantee you can get by with the same approach you might use with colleagues in your own neck of the woods. Much of your cross-culture work will be done in English, but the challenge is to make yourself and your staff understood to non-native English speakers.

Staff will be most successful if they speak or write simply. Avoid jargon, slang, idiomatic expressions, analogies, and metaphors. Watch out for too much reference to US norms and lifestyles. Use humor sparingly and make sure it does not poke fun at any culture (Zielinski, 1998).

Your job, as the leader, is to ensure cultural sensitivity has been ingrained in the communication competencies of all staff working across borders. As with all we've discussed in this book, you must model the way. Begin now to fine-tune your cross-cultural communication savvy.

Communication becomes more complex as organizations break down structures and employ more technology. It won't matter how fantastic your ideas are if you can't communicate them. And, we predict leaders won't be able to communicate adequately without becoming adept at the new skills we've described. Box 3.7 summarizes the old communication patterns you should diminish and the new ones to add to your repertoire, as you employ "The communication exchange: limited and infor-mational for shared and persuasive." To learn more about communicating effectively, read our inter-view with Connie M. Steward, Executive Vice-President, Forum Corporation.

> *It won't matter how fantastic your ideas are if you can't communicate them.*

>> BOX 3.7 **The communication exchange: limited and informational for shared and persuasive**

Stop	Start
1 Informing rather than persuading.	1 Thinking of yourself as a salesperson.
2 Ignoring technological tools or using them incorrectly.	2 Cranking up your technosmarts.
3 Undermanaging communication content and dissemination.	3 Setting communication standards.
4 Undercommunicating the most important stuff.	4 Getting buy-in through participation and ownership.
5 Faking it.	5 Listening more.
6 Thinking locally.	6 Thinking globally.

LEADER PROFILE

A star communicator

Connie M. Steward
Executive Vice-President, Forum Corporation

Connie M. Steward manages Forum Corporation's largest division, servicing US-based and global clients with training and consultative services. She has developed an uncanny ability to communicate persuasively, even when the message is met with resistance.

Q *In our research, we have discovered that effective leaders utilize a great deal of persuasive, not only informative, communication. How do you go about communicating with your staff and others in the organization, particularly in times of change?*

A This is a really important aspect of communication. Both the company, Forum, and I are careful about linking people into the emotional core of our organization. With so many people working remotely, it is critical that they have this linkage. In times of change, you must ratchet-up the amount of communication. In the absence of information, staff will make up information to fill in. So, I use e-mail, voice mail and face-to-face communication, saying "Here's as much as I know." It is extremely important to be truthful, giving the good news as well as the not-so-good news. I try to help people deal with the "point of pride" by explaining what's happening in the organization but, also, *why* the events are so significant. For example, if we're undertaking a strategic initiative that may not be popular, I could draw upon situations where we successfully started our approach and discussed why it worked out so well. Since information gets out so fast via e-mail and voice mail, I meet with staff quickly so they can ask questions and we can dialogue. We also post information about change on our Web site.

Q *How do you deal with resistance to the message?*

A I take resistance really seriously. There must be a venue for staff to share frustrations. I do this in a number of ways. I invite staff to call me with questions. I reach out to people individually, one by one, to try to make sense of what the change means to them. I clarify any inaccurate perceptions. Change is not just about what you think, but also, how you *feel*. When there is an emotional component, the response must be personalized to be effective. I always go back to the client experience and emphasize how the change benefits them.

Q *What communication channels do you use for what purposes? When might you choose electronic communication vs. face-to-face?*

A What I see is the merging of education and information dissemination. I sponsored research a couple of years ago on when to use what communication channel and educational methods. It gives us a logic to work with. To solely inform, we use videoconferencing technology that allows us to see someone's face and hear the message, then key-in questions. To lead to high levels of commitment, leaders must be in the room. Videoconferencing is not effective in this situation. I hold meetings (of the entire division and others) of one hundred people or more, off-site, once each year to ensure staff understand the business strategy of the coming year. Some people ask me why I do this, given the expense. I do it to get hearts and minds around the strategy. Refinement and translation of the strategy into people's work require daily informal communications. To stay in touch on a daily basis, I use e-mail and voice mail. E-mail is a great way to ask for advice, providing instantaneous responses around a key issue. To really engage people, face-to-face communication is necessary.

Q *How do you go about motivating and inspiring others through your communication style? What have you found inspires others?*

A Years ago I did research on what inspires. If you ask people what's most important in leadership, they say investment in the development of their talents and capabilities. A leader must see things from their staffs' perspectives. Where will your staff be when they pick up your electronic message? How will they most likely respond, positively or negatively? The message must be personalized – what does this mean to each staff member? Persuasion doesn't always mean you have to be charismatic. Often the encouraging, quietly supportive, and insightful comments inspire great performance. Then, you have to balance the amount of asking and telling. I deliberately ask for advice and listen. UFO messages – when you don't have any idea where they are coming from – will build frustration. They come out of the blue, without context which is crucial for a message to be understood. I also like to tell stories about the history and legacy of the organization. New staff, particularly, like to hear this. I also like to talk about how others have figured out ways to be successful; here's what they did, what we thought about, and what the outcome was.

Q *How do you communicate with remote staff? Teleconference? Audioconference? How do you stage those events to make them effective?*

A We have an 8.30 am conference call that all are expected to participate in. I use it to update staff on company developments and what we've learned from, for example, an engagement in the UK. We are increasingly using teleconferencing in client situations with our global teams. Staging is extremely important for effective teleconferencing. Preparation is important, as well as skill, in staging multi-cultural conferences. Because we connect with one another via technology doesn't guarantee we reach the multi-cultural audience. Motivation and persuasion is twice the challenge with teleconferences. People can put on the mute button!

Q *What advice would you give other leaders about communicating in their organizations? Dos and don'ts?*

A Leaders need to appreciate that a big part of leadership is learning and helping others to learn. How does each communication you engage in add to the learning for others and yourself? Recognize, too, that how others make sense of information is largely symbolic, through actions. People notice and appreciate when I can model and act consistently with what they believe I should be doing. Leaders can make a big mistake when they assume others hear things the same way they do. Staging communication means thinking about how others will experience your message. Hearts and minds are captured through communication that does not focus solely on financial, statistical information. I would also add that sound-bites communicate most effectively. Brevity and clarity are often better than long, detailed voice mails. Learn how to "net out" your message with succinctness and extreme clarity. Be a good manager of communication. News spreads fast; get on top of it. Do the unexpected from time to time. For example, an eight-year-old sister of one of our staff members was visiting and I asked her to drop me a voice message about what she had learned. I played her message at the opening of a meeting inviting people to a conference for our entire consulting organization. It was impactful and memorable. Being relevant really matters. In today's environment of speed, the more you can frame a message to be immediately relevant and memorable, the better. Sometimes people forget that their voice is so powerful. Communication is not just words, but how the message comes across.

REFERENCES

Cohen, S. (1996) "Mail etiquette and tips," *Training and Development*, 50 (8), 48.

Dixon, G. (1998) "Table-top audio conferencing systems," *Presentations*, 12 (4), 77–81.

Hanke, J. (1998) "Can technology save you from meeting hell?," *Presentations*, 12 (7), 36–44.

Hartman, D. and Nantz, K. (1995) "Send the right messages about e-mail," *Training and Development*, 49 (5), 60.

Hequet, M. (1994) "How telecommuting transforms work," *Training*, 31 (11), 57–61.

Kotter, J. P. (1995) "Leading change: Why transformation efforts fail," *Harvard Business Review*, 73 (2), 59.

Larkin, T.J. and Larkin, S. (1994) *Communicating Change. Winning Employee Support for New Business Goals*. New York: McGraw-Hill.

Lindstrom, R. (1998) "Presentation intelligence: The evolution of presentations in the new enterprise," *Presentations*, 12 (10), 1–22.

Nevis, E. C., Lancourt, J., and Vassallo, H. G. (1996) *Intentional Revolutions*. San Francisco: Jossey-Bass Publishers.

Rothwell, S. (1996) "Satisfaction and participation – Do they matter?," *Manager Update*, 8 (2), 20–32.

Sabath, A. (1998) *Business Etiquette. 101 Ways to Conduct Business With Charm and Savvy*. Franklin Lakes, NJ: Career Press.

"Tangible benefits of videoconferencing," The New Way to Office. Kinko's, 1 (2).

Vander Houwen, B. (1997) "Less Talking, More Listening," *HRMagazine*, 42 (8), 53–9.

Zielinski, D. (1998) "Going Global," *Presentations*, 12 (10), 42–8.

THE WORKFORCE EXCHANGE

Core and permanent for non-core and contract

S am Oslund, manager of domestic violence programs for a mid-sized suburban county, has just completed an analysis of his staffs' workloads and reviewed the organization's strategic plan for the next three years. Noting several key initiatives in which his department will play a major role, Sam has decided that he needs more staff to deliver the outcomes expected of him. He pulls together his team to identify the key jobs that will need to get done and to estimate the number of full-time positions required. Eventually, he will develop several job descriptions that will be the basis for adding new full-time positions. Additionally, Sam figures he'll contract with a temporary agency to plug the holes the two full-time positions can't quite fill and to supplement the weak performance of one of his current staff members. He makes a quick call to the Compensation and Benefits Department to check on salary ranges and benefit costs these positions will entail. He wonders if he can make the full financial commitment at this time, given the upcoming county elections and potential funding cuts for human services.

THE PITFALLS IN WORKFORCE CONFIGURATION AND MANAGEMENT

Sam has just fallen into the classic trap of using old behaviors and thought patterns. Specifically, he has succumbed to an old model of recruiting and a stagnant use of talent in his organization. By thinking of his staff as primarily core and permanent, he has boxed himself into a staff configuration that will not be flexible enough to meet the changing demands of the 21st-century work environment. Who knows if his organization's strategic plan will be valid, given the rapidly changing political and social conditions that surround his work environment? Can he really develop his core staff members' skills fast enough to meet the demands of the changing environment, not to mention technological advances?

It's not that what he's doing is entirely wrong; it's just that Sam is not considering an alternative which may give him more flexibility. He needs to take a serious look at his leadership approach with his workforce and stop doing certain behaviors and initiate others. We call this "The workforce exchange: core and permanent for non-core and contract."

STOP DOING THESE THINGS

1 Stop creating obsolete job descriptions

Before we suggest using job descriptions for kindling, let's take a detour. Remember the book *In Search of Excellence* by Tom Peters and Robert Waterman (1982)? It was a catalyst for eventually re-writing the concept of customer service. It taught us that good customer service required organizations give up their inflexible structures to better accommodate customers' needs for high quality and speedy responsiveness.

Job descriptions have set up rigid boundaries into which work assignments are made to fit. Today's organizations cry out for more integration among their components, as well as more flexibility to use staff members as needs arise. Just as customer service didn't improve until organizations gave up their stiff and unbending structures, leaders must relinquish their firm hold on job descriptions that promote territoriality and a rigid who-does-what philosophy.

2 Stop developing so many full-time, permanent positions

Don't get locked into staffing patterns you can't easily undo. Because of fast-changing market conditions coupled with the need to manage costs tightly, it is critical that organizations maintain as small a core workforce as possible to be nimble enough to stay competitive and viable.

> *Whenever you believe you need to employ someone, stop, look, and listen. Don't automatically hire to existing job descriptions.*

Stop thinking with a "permanent" mentality. Whenever you believe you need to employ someone, stop, look, and listen. Don't automatically hire to existing job descriptions. Examine the work that needs to be done, asking yourself, "Will it still be there in one year? Will your current staff have the skills needed to perform it at the expected level? Will the training you would have to provide to existing staff take too much time and expense?"

3 Stop treating part-time, temporary, and contract staff as peripheral

A study conducted by Feldman, Doerpinghaus, and Turnley (1994) in *Organizational Dynamics* identified the key concerns of temporary staffs. They reported being discouraged by the dehumanizing and impersonal ways they are treated. "I have been approached on a new assignment with 'Hey you, I order you today' to which I replied, 'My name is Wendy, but I am not a hamburger'" (p. 49), said one of the workers interviewed. Temps also crave more security in their positions and want better insurance and pension benefits. They also claim employers fail to provide an accurate picture of their job assignments. Most feel their skills are not fully utilized (i.e. they are underemployed.)

Stop thinking of your permanent staff as the only ones capable of doing important, front-and-center tasks. Avoid treating non-core staff as if they are appendages to your work unit. Remember, non-core doesn't mean non-essential; it may mean that contracted staff have a special niche needed for your business – a niche that may not be practical or efficient for you to cultivate with your permanent staff. So, stop giving them all the "grunt work" that no one else wants. The specific talents of many non-core staff, especially in technical fields, are sorely needed in organizations. These people can literally go anywhere for employment. They'll likely quit if they are left to the uninteresting tasks.

Then, remember that non-core staff are part of your team and deserve their fair share of credit for work well done. Stop singling out only the core, permanent staff when rewards and recognition are due. Remember that everyone is critical to the success of your organization.

We heard from one leader who reported that his boss was operating in a way that she thought was sensitive to the needs of the non-core workforce. Typically, she met with the non-core group separately from the core group to make sure she was successfully fielding their questions and meeting their specific needs. We strongly suggest that the leader stop doing this because it does not promote project teamwork between core and non-core.

What about orientation and training? Try this exercise. Walk to the group responsible for bringing on new staff members and ask to see the job titles of individuals attending their sessions. We predict that practically all the individuals attending will be your core, permanent staff. Who's training and orienting the non-core staff? Remember, many of these individuals are interacting with your key customers, vendors, and/or stakeholders. And, if they *are* being trained, you'll likely find them in separate classes. This is not an effective way to integrate the non-core staff into your business. At Lawson Software training classes include vendors, suppliers, contractors, customers, and the core staff. Many of our interviewees indicated this is a superb way to blend non-core staff into the culture of their organizations. Training is not just about learning a technical discipline or a specific topic, but about discovering what makes an organization tick. Successful leaders have stopped treating their non-core staff as appendages when it comes to involvement in training events.

This "stop" is summarized by Diana Salesky, a communication consultant to American Express:

> *Unlike the practices of American Express, some organizations make you feel as though you're not part of the organizational team. They do this by being stingy with information, making borderline rude remarks about consultants, and generally making you feel excluded from the mainstream of activity. This is very different from my experiences at American Express where they want you to give your opinion and really hear it. This makes me want to contribute more. American Express has the long-term contract relationships to prove how successful this is.*

4 Stop undermanaging non-core staff performance

We found that some leaders are reluctant to make tough calls when it comes to managing the performance of non-core staff. One leader related a scenario in which his project team leader had to provide negative performance feedback to her team of core and non-core staff. This is what she said to her core staff:

> *This project went off schedule because you didn't use me as a resource to help influence some other key decision makers. I hold you accountable for this because it was your responsibility to keep me informed. In the future, I need you to be more responsive about using me to help you out.*

By contrast, this is what he heard her say to one of the non-core team members working on this project, "I'll bet you're relieved that you don't have to get all this negative feedback anymore!" Stop thinking that feedback is just for your core staff, particularly when it comes to constructive criticism.

START DOING THESE THINGS

The general principle to follow as you employ the "workforce exchange" is to manage the non-core staff in parallel ways to the core staff. Blur the lines between the two groups of staffs, thinking of them as one, integrated, fine-tuned machine. Start doing these things to make it happen.

> *Blur the lines between the two groups of staffs, thinking of them as one, integrated, fine-tuned machine.*

1 Start identifying the type of non-core staff that best suits your needs

Here are some definitions you may find useful. *Part-time* staff are those who work up to 35 hours per week and often their status continues over time. *Seasonal* staff are hired for a defined period of time, typically when seasonal activities are at their peak. *Temporary* staff are used as substitutes when full-time staff are on leave, ill or vacationing, or during times of heavy workloads or new start-ups. Most often they are hired through temporary agencies. Another option is *employee leasing.* Through leasing companies, staff can be hired for longer-term assignments with the leasing company providing benefits, managing the payroll, and doing the hiring. The leasor supervises the employee. *Independent contractors* are paid for a specific project or days of service based on their skills. Independent contractors manage their own taxes and benefits since they are not staff members. Yet another option to consider is *students* (undergraduate or graduate) who may be in need of internships to complete their degree requirements or co-op students in programs that alternate work and study (McKie and Lipsett, 1995). Some of them may have sophisticated skills. For example, at the University of St Thomas, Department of Organization Learning and Development, many part-time graduate students are vice-presidents, managers, and specialists in the companies for which they work. Yet, they must fulfill internship requirements.

2 Start deciding what you want non-core staff to do

Remember the list of typical tasks organizations are assigning to non-core staff (*see* Chapter 2, Box 2.4)? These will help you be more specific in designing project/work descriptions you can use for recruiting. Think about the specific work assignment and activities you want performed, the length of the assignment, and the types of skills the project must have.

If you want to design a competitive bidding process for individuals or organizations in which to engage, develop a detailed Request for Proposal (RFP). This is standard procedure for government organizations. Many corporations have begun to use a similar process to identify the best candidates for a given assignment by utilizing the proposal to provide a more detailed written description of the contractor's skills and approach to a given assignment.

Outsourcing agencies typically use a standard form. In an article in *Personnel*, Sunoo and Laabs (1994) recommend scrapping it and developing your own instead to ensure it meets your needs. Box 4.1 displays an example of a template for a performance contract, outlining some of the components you should include.

One caution. Non-core staff will potentially have access to a wide range of information within your organization. Secure all information you do not want them to have and be very clear about confidentiality requirements. One organization we know asks its temporary CPAs to undergo a professional ethics exam before contracting with them.

3 Start recruiting and orienting non-core staff as carefully as core staff

Begin by allowing plenty of time to search out alternatives and interview both firms and individuals carefully. Be selective in choosing agencies, looking for those that specialize in the type of staff persons you need and that understand the nuances of work assignments and needed job skills. Choose those organizations that have stability in their labor pools, rather than rapid turnover. This will ensure their staff have performed reasonably well over time. Ask about the amount of training the agency provides. Those that take care to develop their staff through educational programs, tuition reimbursement, or self-paced training opportunities are most likely to provide the best talent. As a general rule of thumb, it is best to work with a small number of agencies with whom you've developed a

>> BOX 4.1 **Performance contract template**

1 A clear explanation of the work assignment, including "deliverables" – the products you expect as an outcome of the work.

Products might include a report with recommendations on ways to solve given problems, a software program, an on-line help-desk function for computer problems, the design and delivery of a training program, a solution to a given technical problem.

2 A delineation of roles and responsibilities of the contractor vs. your organization.

Roles and responsibilities might include who provides what kind of information, whose equipment is to be used, who holds the copyright for written documents created, who does the performance review.

3 A reporting schedule.

This might entail how frequently progress reports/meetings will be held and who should be involved.

4 An indication of where the work will be done.

Will the work be performed in your offices/work site or at the contractor's site, or both? Will an office be provided for the contractor?

5 A statement of penalties that may be assessed.

If work is not completed according to the standards and time frames agreed upon, will penalties be assessed? What will they be?

6 An indication of the duration of the contract.

How long will the contractor be working with your organization?

7 A clearly delineated payment schedule.

Will payment be made as each task/project is completed or after a specific period of time? Is payment subject to approval of the work?

8 A statement of confidentiality requirements.

Note: Please consult your legal department or attorney to ensure all aspects of the contract meet with your organization's legal requirements.

Put these components into contracts you develop with non-core staff and agencies.

close relationship and who understand your organization's culture and needs (Feldman, Doerpinghaus, and Turnley, 1994). Don't turn all control over to the agency. Interview candidates yourself before accepting them to work in your organization. Box 4.2 provides questions to ask agencies that you are considering using for your staffing needs.

>> BOX 4.2   **Questions to ask employment agencies**

- What is your history in placing the type of staff persons we are asking for?
- How do you go about recruiting staff members? Through professional organizations? Newspapers? Word of mouth? Internet?
- How do you interview prospective staff persons? What are some of the interview questions you use?
- How do you know what staff persons' skills and abilities are? What evidence do you look for?
- How do you train your labor pool?
- What is the average length of time staff persons in the category we are looking for have worked with your agency?
- What kind of incentives do you provide?
- What kind of benefits do you offer?
- What kind of contract do you use?
- If a staff person you place with an organization is not performing, how do you typically handle the situation?
- What do you expect from the organizations who contract with you?

These questions will provide a vehicle for ensuring the contracting agency plays a key leadership role with the non-core staff. The questions will also assist you in targeting the best possible employment agency for your organization.

When looking for individuals or independent contractors, part-timers, or students, use the same systematic approach you would for core staff. Use a variety of recruiting modes, including the Internet – a source of candidates many organizations are discovering is invaluable for recruiting both core and non-core staff.

Develop interview questions that test your contractors' specialty skills. As you would with your permanent, core staff, test their fit to your organization's mission, values, and beliefs, ascertaining their capacity to be a team player. Choose the right people for the right reasons. Remember the competencies of effective non-core staff members we described in Chapter 2, Box 2.5? We've developed some interview questions (*see* Box 4.3) to probe for those competencies to help you screen candidates and make the best choices for your given needs.

Once you have found them, bring non-core staff on-board with style. Make sure you create orientation programs that make your non-core staff feel respected, valued, and part of the team. Your goal: make them feel wanted and bond them quickly to the organization and team members. Involve your core staff in developing and delivering the orientation. Consider using a "buddy" system, pairing core staff with non-core staff to provide ongoing assistance. In many cases, given you have an orientation program in place for your core staff, you may not have to create much that is new – simply put the non-core staff through the same routine. When the assignments are short, have in hand a condensed version of the full-fledged orientation packet that can be reviewed quickly with short-stay staff persons, or consider delivering it on-line to those working from a remote site too far away to make on-site orientation practical. Be prepared with the correct tools and materials for non-core staff so they can hit

> *Make sure you create orientation programs that make your non-core staff feel respected, valued, and part of the team.*

>> BOX 4.3   **Interview questions to ask potential non-core staff**

- What is your work background?

- What work experiences and skills qualify you to do this work for us?

- Develop several scenarios to "test" knowledge, for example:
  - For an Information Systems help-line contractor: "If a call came to you on our help line regarding how to create a default template on Microsoft Word, how would you respond?"
  - When you've been confronted with an angry customer in the past, how have you responded?"

- Develop several scenarios to "test" interpersonal skills:
  - "Given you would be working with us on-site one day each week, what would you do to develop effective working relationships with your team mates?"
  - "What have you done to develop effective team relationships in other organizations you have worked for?"

- What equipment do you have available in your off-site location (if applicable)? What would you expect us to provide?

- What do you like best and least about part-time/temporary/contract work?

- What do you know about our organization? What would you like to know in order to work with us effectively?

- What would you expect of us to establish a good working relationship?

the ground running. If they are working off-site, be sure the location is properly equipped. Box 4.4 lists critical components in non-core staff orientation.

>> BOX 4.4   **Components in non-core staff orientation**

- Background on your organization: products or services, customers, mission, strategic goals, core values.

- Tour of facilities.

- Review of organizational policies and procedures.

- Review of work procedures:
  - if on-site: clocking in and out, breaks, lunches.
  - if off-site: checking in on-line, by phone or fax.

- Orientation to use of equipment, tools.

- Team-building exercises with core staff.

- Review of benefits and incentives as applicable.

- Training schedule and opportunities.

Notice that these are virtually the same components needed for orienting your core staff. That's the point – treat all staff with the same practices.

As consultants, we serve as non-core staff in our client organizations. When hired as a consultant by Mayo Clinic, Dr Essex was asked to complete a two-day orientation program, at her expense, which included an in-depth review of the history and core values of the organization, a tour, and several books on the background of Mayo. She was questioned by her client, Human Resource Strategist, Robert Blomberg, about the orientation to ensure her understanding of the culture. While time consuming, the experience has proved invaluable in being able to deliver relevant training and consulting advice. Similarly, Dr Kusy was asked to attend a two-day organization-wide orientation to a team development process at one of his client sites in preparation to assist them in developing a strategic plan.

4 Start actively managing non-core staff performance

Coach your non-core staff with the same performance management process you would use for core staff. Remember the basics:

- review work expectations, performance standards, measurement methods, and time lines at the onset of non-core staff person's work with your organization;

- set up periodic check points for reviewing work, giving feedback, and problem solving as needed;

- review the result at the end of each assignment, giving praise and constructive criticism as the outcome warrants;

- decide up front the communication mode you will use to manage performance as well as the frequency of interaction desired by both parties (*see* Chapter 3 for guidelines on communicating with e-mail, fax, phone and face-to-face).

If you are working with agencies to place staff in your organization, make sure to include them in the performance management process both in terms of the agencies' performance as well as the individual staff members they are placing with you.

In spite of your best attempts, performance problems may crop up with individuals or agencies. Be alert for the five most common issues you may face. First, you could discover the skills of your non-core staff are not adequate to meet the requirements of the performance contract. The work quality is simply not at desirable levels, requiring too much coaching and training for the scope of the contract. Implied here is that you or an agency you employ did not effectively screen for the staff members' skill levels.

A second issue could be that the non-core staff person, most likely one working remotely, is not available enough for you to feel you can monitor their work. E-mail or voice mail is not answered promptly, making you wonder if they are really being accountable to the work assignment, team, and organization. It may be that you did not lay out adequate expectations for availability as we suggested earlier or they do not have the skills or abilities to work independently.

A third situation that could crop up is conflict created by non-core staff being unfriendly, disengaged, or disrespectful to core staff. Perhaps your interview questions did not probe well enough in the areas of interpersonal and team membership skills. When it occurs, this problem must be addressed quickly to avoid ugly team dynamics and low morale.

Making political blunders by being insensitive to the culture of the host organization is a fourth problem area that non-core staff could exhibit. Check your orientation process to ensure they are receiving adequate information about the "dos and don'ts" of working successfully in your organization.

Violations of confidentiality and privacy of information may present a fifth problem. Ensure the performance contract, when relevant, spells out clear expectations and that your information systems are properly equipped to protect proprietary information.

Box 4.5 provides a summary of the five most common performance issues of non-core staff. Tackle these issues just as you would for core staff. Identify the gap between the performance expectation and the performance being delivered. Have a feedback discussion. While common management wisdom rules that face-to-face communication is the preferred mode for feedback, non-core staff who work off-site may have to be dealt with via phone or even e-mail. Remember, you most likely hired non-core staff for added flexibility. This goes both ways; leaders must demonstrate their versatility, in return, by occasionally foregoing their typical face-to-face performance dialogues. For more serious discussions, we still recommend face-to-face communication even if it requires footing the bill for travel expenses. Once the feedback is

---

▶▶ BOX 4.5 **Potential performance issues of non-core staff**

- Skills not adequate to meet the requirements of the performance contract.
- Not being accountable by being unavailable. E-mail or voice mail not answered promptly.
- Creating conflict with core staff by being unfriendly, disengaged, or disrespectful.
- Making political blunders by being insensitive to the culture of the host organization.
- Violations of confidentiality and privacy of information.

These are the five most common performance issues non-core staff may exhibit. Be alert for them.

delivered, jointly agree on a solution and a date by which the change will be made. Follow up flawlessly. If you don't see improvement, move to terminate the contract expeditiously. Capitalize on the advantages of non-core staff. You are not wedded to them. You hired them to gain flexibility. You expected high performance. Don't settle for anything less.

> *You expected high performance. Don't settle for anything less.*

To complete the performance management process, remember to motivate and reward non-core staff. Make them feel as important as you know they are. When hosting recognition events, make sure they are fully included and involved in the awards and accolades you give out. As a general rule of thumb, avoid calling temporary staff persons "temps"; use their names instead. Make sure they are included in meetings, receive all relevant communication, and are invited to social events. Keep them interested by giving them challenging assignments and asking for their input in the decision-making process (Caudron, 1995).

Some organizations are including sales force and home office staff in their financial incentives programs. In its early stages, before its initial public offering (IPO), Life USA Holding, Inc. gave field agents 15 percent of their commissions in stock to motivate them to help the company grow. In addition, home office staff took 10 percent of their compensation to purchase stock. Other companies are sharing profit and bonuses proportionally with their non-core staff.

Don't insist on rigid hours. Remember, you've set measurable outcomes for the work assignment. It's up to the staff person to figure out how to meet them. They may have other assignments for other organizations they are working on and need to juggle their schedules accordingly. Let go of the reins, using the strategies we've outlined to manage, not control, performance.

Box 4.6 provides a summary of "The workforce exchange: core and permanent for non-core and contract." Begin now to cast off any old thinking patterns and behaviors you may have acquired related to your organization's need for increasing numbers of permanent staff. Embrace the flexibility you'll gain, as well as specialized skills, when you welcome increasing numbers of non-core staff.

Now, read what Maggie Gagliardi, Senior Vice-President of Executive Resources and Staffing at American Express discussed in our interview with her concerning utilizing a flexible workforce.

> ➤➤ BOX 4.6 **The workforce exchange: core and permanent for non-core and contract**

Stop	Start
1 Creating obsolete job descriptions.	1 Identifying the type of non-core staff that best suits your needs.
2 Developing so many full-time, permanent positions.	2 Deciding what you want non-core staff to do.
3 Treating part-time, temporary, and contract staff as peripheral.	3 Recruiting and orienting non-core staff as carefully as core staff.
4 Undermanaging non-core staff performance.	4 Actively managing non-core staff performance.

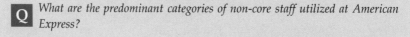

LEADER PROFILE

A versatile leader

Maggie Gagliardi
Senior Vice-President, Executive Resources and Staffing, American Express

Maggie Gagliardi is a leader who integrates visionary and practical approaches in gearing her organization's workforce for the 21st century. She successfully positions contract and outsourced staff to help American Express better achieve its goals. You'll hear answers to questions many leaders have about the best ways to lead effectively a very divergent, flexible workforce.

Q *What are the predominant categories of non-core staff utilized at American Express?*

A While not all organizations make the same distinctions as we do, our two primary groups are contractors and outsourced staff. Our contractors work primarily on-site, such as a temporary secretary who supports a business unit or a lead programmer in technology. Outsourced staff are not generally housed in our facilities, but still perform a needed service, such as a telephone service representative who works at another site.

Q *How do you orient and train these non-core staff?*

A The bottom line is that anyone who works for us has to perform at a level commensurate with the American Express brand. We expect this from our own staff, and we have the same standard for those who are not formally a part of American Express. To make this happen, we use a number of strategies. First of all, we hire people for a specific skill and the experiences they have. So, functional training isn't always needed. Second, for departments that use a high number of contract staff, our leaders coach and mentor, as appropriate. Third, our own staff orient and train these individuals to the kind of service level we expect.

Q *How do you involve these individuals in teams?*

A They could be involved in team meetings, depending upon the need. We may also invite them to town hall meetings and other types of information-sharing events, if relevant. This is critical because you have to be cautious not to misrepresent them in the organization – they are legally not employees of ours and it is a misrepresentation to treat them as such. However, this should not mean you treat them as second-class. You want them to feel an affiliation with your organization and feel part of the team they are working with. If you don't, you'll reduce the chances of getting the most successful results. You want them to do the best on your behalf.

Q *What kinds of rewards are used?*

A Basically, while these are taken care of by the vendor, we have also found it very effective to present them with small, meaningful gifts indicating our appreciation for their work, such as movie tickets. And, if someone deserves an additional reward beyond this, we certainly discuss this with the vendor.

Q *Why might you bring these individuals in vs. core staff?*

A The answer to this depends on what we need. First, we might need a unique or special skill that we currently do not have. Second, because of fluctuating workforce requirements, we look for people who can manage projects during times when our business needs more people. Third, we have short-term situations, when we're in a crunch and would need someone to help us during a specific emergency.

Q *What other strategies have been useful in working with these individuals?*

A One, in particular, comes to mind. We have designed and published guidelines to help our leaders in working with contractors. We cover

➤

> such topics as the role of the contract person, hiring of former employees, billing, contractor fees, participation in AmEx events, rewards, training, involvement in informal celebrations, and key accountabilities. This helps our leaders think about how best to manage this part of our workforce. Again, while these contractors and outsourced staff are legally separate from our organization, the trick is almost to strike up a partnership with them where they want to deliver the performance and service expected of the American Express brand.

REFERENCES

Caudron, S. (1995) "Are temps doing their best?," *Personnel*, 74 (11), 32–8.

Feldman, D. C., Doerpinghaus, H. I., and Turnley, W. H. (1994) "Managing temporary workers: A permanent HRM challenge," *Organizational Dynamics*, 23 (2), 49.

McKie, G. and Lipsett, L. (1995) *The Contingent Worker: A Human Resource Perspective*. Alexandria, VA: Society for Human Resource Management.

Peters, T. and Waterman, R. (1982) *In Search of Excellence: Lessons from America's Best-Run Companies*. New York: Harper & Row.

Sunoo, B. and Laabs, J. (1994) "Winning strategies for outsourcing contracts," *Personnel Journal*, 73 (3), 69–78.

THE RECOGNITION EXCHANGE

Single-generational for multi-generational focus

J avit Rashatar is one of those remarkable leaders who not only keeps up to date on state-of-the-art leadership practices, but also applies the best of what he reads. Lately, he's been reading so much about the different generations in the workforce today that he believes it's just "media hype, over-propaganda, and a bit of a fad." To Javit, this is all about people whining because they're not being catered to or it's just over-stereotyping each generation.

Javit's response to the generational perspectives in the workforce today is to treat each staff person fairly. To him, this means a number of things, such as individually meeting with each of his direct reports for one hour per week. He judiciously schedules these "one-on-one" meetings so that there is concentrated time to focus on key issues and plan future directions. Javit relishes these opportunities to mentor team members; he knows that everyone really appreciates these individually focused times.

He also treats each of his team members equitably by rewarding outstanding performers with the standard 5 percent salary increase, solid performers with a 4 percent increase, and you know how the rest of this tale goes. Javit has never had any complaints about this process, particularly because he spells out very specifically the performance he's looking for.

In addition, the "fairness factor" comes into play as Javit rewards his team members with movement "up" the career ladder. Everyone wants to get ahead, he figures, and he's going to provide vehicles for doing this – even if it means pushing individuals into other departments. Javit believes that this strategy should also reduce the probability that team members will leave the organization.

Unfortunately, each of these efforts is about to backfire in some way. Javit is going to be hit between the eyes.

FAIR DOESN'T MEAN GOOD FOR ALL

From our interviews with world leaders, we learned some interesting perspectives relating to Javit's dilemma. Some of you may be saying, "What dilemma?" It's the situation where everyone gets the same; neither deviations nor substitutions allowed. We have found that this is not how successful leaders manage and reward performance. They have told us that each of the generations may be asking for different performance incentives. For some, the regularly scheduled one-on-one meeting is way too formal and largely overkill. Some want time with the leader but in shorter intervals, more frequently, and on an as-needed basis. Others want concentrated, uninterrupted, quality time.

When rewarding performance, some outstanding achievers are less concerned with money and more with development opportunities. Others want a bigger piece of the organization's financial return than what the standard salary increase can provide. What happens in many organizations is that some individuals get reinforced with rewards they really don't want. Some staff are rewarded with movement up the career ladder. Everyone isn't necessarily looking up. Some want lateral opportunities, not "ladderal." Others want recognition by coaching others, not always moving up.

Let's set the record straight. Yes, there has been over-stereotyping of generational differences in the workforce. Sometimes, this has a tendency to turn into clichés without a lot of substance. Leaders do have an inclination to manage and reward performance based on what *they* find personally motivating. Successful leaders are able to separate the myths from reality.

While the year someone was born certainly does not tell everything about him or her, it may help explain some things. Why is this so important? A generation is formed through a set of common experiences that are starting points for action. Understanding this serves as a context to begin discussions about what's motivating for people. Successful leaders who have done this report an amazing sense of connecting with others, as well as improved performance just a notch higher than they had expected.

To motivate others, successful leaders sometimes set aside their own agenda and use a varied approach of rewarding performance. This chapter will help you determine what you'll need to do to establish this smorgasbord of performance reward approaches: "The recognition exchange: single-generational for multi-generational focus."

GENERATION X, BABY BOOMER, AND TRADITIONALIST: ONE MOTIVATIONAL STYLE IS NOT BEST

In Chapter 2 we provided a synopsis of these three generations. Generation Xers were born from approximately 1964 through 1975. The term "generation X" was initially coined because individuals studying these new entrants into the workforce did not see them as having a common identity like other age groups, hence the term "X." As time went on, some common threads for this generation became evident. There are 45 percent fewer of them than the baby boomers who were born from 1946 through 1963. The term "baby boomer" originated from the tremendous birth boom that occurred post-World War II (Sterling and Waite, 1998). The traditionalists were born from 1925 through 1945.

In order effectively to motivate staff members from all three generations, you'll have to give up the following approaches.

STOP DOING THESE THINGS

1 Stop squeezing the motivation out of generation Xers

Early in the study of this age group, people labeled them as "slack-offs" and "wayward spirits," without a sense of direction or commitment to an organization. We'd like to dispel this notion by helping you understand what really makes them "tick." Then, you'll be well-positioned to stop generic incentives that are likely to put a choke hold on their motivational spirit.

Growing up as latchkey kids, Xers are fiercely autonomous and relish activities that are self-paced and independent. So, it stands to reason, they often have a hard time with excessive groupwork, such as meetings and team-building activities. While these may certainly be necessary at times, you'll need to determine which are most essential and stop the superfluous ones. If you don't, these people will go elsewhere because they have quickly discovered the world is their oyster as jobs are in plentiful supply while talent is not. One example of what to stop is the Tuesday staff meeting, always scheduled at 8.30 am. You know what we're talking about here – the meeting many don't really want to be at. Xers largely see this as politicking and group-process time. If you don't need the meeting for interactive activities and it's just for "FYI," then cancel it and use much less expensive vehicles, i.e. e-mail, to inform. You'll need to stop those high-control activities that make Xers jump out of their cubes and run. This is the first generation technologically connected to computers (or "wired" as they call it), allowing them opportunities to multi-task and get to an end result in a variety of different ways.

You'll also need to eliminate those systems steeped in needless paper-work and processes. Some of you may be saying that we should get rid of this stuff anyway! While maybe true, it's the Xer who is likely to react most negatively. Even though some of them may be needed, we're talking about ending procedures based on exceptions rather than everyday prac-tices. For example, are all those approval signatures really needed? Does it make sense to require triplicate forms?

As generation X gyrates around start-up opportunities and gradually assumes more responsible positions, they do become more committed to careers than researchers once thought. However, they see "career" in a dif-ferent light from other generations. They are not necessarily motivated by jobs focusing on movement up the career ladder. So leaders should stop trying to motivate them with upward-looking symbolic rewards connected to organizational status.

High control coupled with excessive hierarchy with this group erodes teamwork and trust. At a national sales meeting, a VP of Marketing invited all sales managers and associates to a week-long meeting in a beautiful resort town on the East Coast. As everyone began to arrive, one sales man-ager was amazed that associates were upset because management had private rooms and associates had to share rooms. The VP of Marketing lis-tened and responded with her own revised "seating plan" for future meetings. Xers really disdain the two-stage hierarchical structure of "we" and "they." We have learned that future-minded leaders have stopped excessively promoting those hierarchical status symbols that significantly erode teamwork and commitment. And with talent in scarce supply, you can't afford to lose quality team players.

2 Stop stagnating the careers of baby boomers

Nothing will deter boomer motivation as much as a deadlocked career. Much more organizationally loyal than Xers, boomers connect to work life even if they don't like their jobs. Xers regard many boomers as workaholics whom they see as frequently placing job above home life.

To boomers, careers become stale when there aren't adequate opportunities to participate in key organizational decisions. Maybe because they grew up during the turbulent "groupie" times of the 1960s, boomers prefer to talk at length through issues more than other generations. So stop cutting them off when they want to take time for this. Denying them opportunities for self- or team discoveries will further alienate them. Don't focus only on giving them the final decision, without some opportunities to gain consensus around an issue.

Having grown up in an environment of relative affluence compared to their parents, many boomers see career as symbolic of prosperity, rewards, and status. They have matured as a result of organizational downsizings, rising unemployment, and a movement towards volunteerism and social responsibility. Surprisingly, amidst their penchant for the finer things in life that money brings, they will probably be the first generation in history not to exceed their parents' retirement incomes (Newman, 1993). There are several reasons for this – unemployment, a "spend" philosophy, little career growth opportunities because there are too many boomers, and a proliferation of college loans.

So when they can't have all the material trappings that money provides, career can become an even more important driver. Stop bulldozing their careers by pigeon-holing them into jobs without a voice and making them accept positions that don't allow them to teach others what they know.

3 Stop cutting off traditionalists from pivotal organizational activities

Traditionalists are audacious in using their past successes as their calling cards. Why not? They have been instrumental in building many organizations. No longer forced to retire, older workers are staying in the workforce longer than any previous group.

In managing traditionalists, leaders need to stop ignoring the valuable contributions they have made to organizations. Loyalty and allegiance are dimensions they themselves say have been largely bypassed and should mean something. Stop removing them from activities that really impact the organization. Some traditionalists have told us they feel they get left on the bench as they age, cut off from the mainstream of activity, with the assumption by their leaders that "You can't teach an old dog new tricks." Be sure you're not making an unfounded assumption that late-career staff can't continue to play a vital role in your organization.

4 Stop thinking everyone wants what you want

In our sample of successful leaders we learned that a pronounced focus on "my way is best" is the sure sign of an arrogant leader. What's motivating for you may not be motivating for others. Look at those stops that have a deleterious effect on your organization and get ready to employ the starts we're about to present.

> **What's motivating for you may not be motivating for others.**

START DOING THESE THINGS

1 Start tapping into Xers' independence and flexibility

Recruit talent quickly and with panache. Search for Xers on-line. The process is simple and inexpensive: a potential recruit "calls up" the appropriate Web page for your company, clicks on the relevant ad, and directly communicates on-line. This will allow for quick identification of candidates within hours instead of the typical three weeks from newspapers. It also gives Xers the message that your organization is technologically savvy, helping you attract the talent that is in scarce supply. With US unemployment at an historic low (Johnson, 1998), leaders will need to do everything possible to attract good workers.

For this generation, don't hire or promote exclusively based on credentials. Realistically, they may not have had enough longevity to build the right credentials. Assess such factors as their energy to problem-solve creatively, manage multiple priorities, and operate with a service orientation. Kathryn Peterson, Senior Human Resources Manager for Andersen Consulting's Minneapolis office, told us about the approach her organization takes:

> *We look for people with a positive, can-do attitude, along with solid analytical skills and a good track record. This shouldn't be based only on the quantity of work experiences, but more on the total picture of the individual.*

We can teach many technical components of the job, but it's very difficult to teach people to have a positive attitude.

When recruiting, don't be afraid to ask what makes work fun. At Schneider Corporation, Tim Fliss, VP of Human Resources, noted how important it is to ask what would make Xers *leave* a company! At the top of the list is often that work is no longer enjoyable. While recruiting entry-level professional positions for a Fortune 500 corporation, Dr Kusy and the interviewing team were amazed at the consistency in the questions Xer recruits asked, such as:

- How does this organization value leisure time?
- What does this organization do to promote balance between work and home?
- Why do you like working here? (Remember, they were asking *us* this question!)
- Are there stated working hours?

Leaders have told us they were initially in a pattern of rejecting individuals because they did not have the "required" organizational commitment. Maggie Gagliardi, Senior Vice-President, Executive Resources and Staffing at American Express, related to us the importance of leaders changing the way they view organizational commitment: "The perspectives that leaders have of reward and recognition need to be changed. It should no longer be an expectation of one career in just one organization."

As some leaders pursued Xer candidates primarily because of the labor shortage and eventually hired them, they were surprised that many of them were stars when given the right rewards and performance management. Gregg Steinhafel, Executive Vice-President of Merchandising for Target Stores, shared how organizational commitment occupies a different place in his organization:

New recruits we hire are more concerned with workplace balance than more seasoned individuals. They are not less committed than people we hired 10 to 20 years ago; they just view the world differently – they are not willing to make as many personal sacrifices as their predecessors.

Innovative leaders in our study spoke passionately about providing opportunities for balance as not only the "right" thing to do, but also a key element in attracting Xers. Organizations promoting work–home balance may not guarantee a set 40-hour week. What they do guarantee is that if you work hard (and yes, sometimes 60 to 70 hours per week), you won't need anyone's "permission" to work significantly less hours at another time. Robert Stevens, President and CEO of Ridgeview Medical Center in Waconia, Minnesota, is helping his organization wrestle with this issue. According to him, "People need a better frame of mind to make the transition between home and work, and vice versa. We encourage them to take breaks to contemplate and meditate. We have seen clashes between newer physicians and older ones because they don't want to work 12-hour days. They recognize they have another life."

With Xers, expect and ask questions during the interviewing process related to work–home balance. According to a 1997 international survey conducted by PricewaterhouseCoopers (formerly Coopers & Lybrand), the

> *Play and work go hand in hand for generation X. To them, there is life after work.*

top priority of 1200 students in 30 leading universities in 10 countries is achieving a balanced lifestyle (Coopers & Lybrand, 1997). Specifically, 45 percent of the respondents ranked the ability to have a satisfying life outside work as the most important factor in determining their first place of employment. This surpassed the second most important variable, building a sound private financial base (33 percent). Play and work go hand in hand for generation X. To them, there *is* life after work.

To help you with recruiting, we've created a checklist of interviewing questions. While you may find some of these questions appropriate for other generations, they will be specifically applicable for this new breed of talent. Box 5.1 provides this road map to successful recruiting.

➤➤ BOX 5.1   Interview questions to ask generation Xers

- What are some of the ways you prefer to juggle multiple priorities?
- What advice could you give about how you prefer to be led?
- How do you balance work and home?
- What kind of flexibility do you need to work most productively?
- How do you use on-line interactions to communicate with others?
- If you could, which work rules you've experienced would you change?
- What kinds of rewards work for you?

Notice that these questions focus on process, not specific tasks. This makes a difference in assessing a full range of Xer skills.

Once Xers have joined your organization and expectations have been established, reward them with independent responsibilities. When setting expectations, don't think this is only the leader's responsibility – consider a collaborative process. Keep an open mind that different doesn't have to mean wrong. Evaluate the outcome, not necessarily the way the project was done.

A dynamic way leaders have told us they gear Xers to independence is to give them opportunities for making presentations to executive management. If Xers are not completely ready for this assignment now, innovative leaders find ways of including them as part of their own presentations to executives. We have learned that leaders who grow high performers often put them on assignments for which they are not quite ready. With adequate assessment of their skills followed by appropriate coaching, Xers will develop more quickly.

Because Xers want to get ahead fast, consider allowing them to jump around your organization on varied lateral assignments. We learned how critical this perspective is at Target Stores from their Executive Vice-President of Merchandising, Gregg Steinhafel: "New team members we hire see many successful developmental paths vs. just one career path. They are still goal-oriented and want to be involved and engaged. They want responsibility as fast as they can get it."

Sometimes these assignments are unwelcomed. If so, coach individuals on how the opportunity offered could set the stage for a myriad of others. For example, share how it may enhance their future marketability, and ultimately, their ability to operate autonomously. If you don't, they're likely to go elsewhere.

One of the first things leaders have noted about some members of this generation is that casualness and, sometimes abruptness, is a by-product of their independence and flexibility. This is most pronounced when you consider that their social skills are not always the best. They can be flippant when handling customers and sometimes don't even address them by name. When interacting within their organization, they may argue a bit too much at an important meeting with a senior leader, or question them more than non-Xers might. To generation X, it's no big deal. To boomers and traditionalists, it's a cause for alarm! To innovative leaders – no matter the generation – it's about style, etiquette, or just a different way of seeing things. Gillian Thomas, Human Resource Manager at Motorola Australia Software Centre, noted her observations of how Xers sometimes challenge the status quo:

Gen X challenges management more than boomers have ever done. "Why? How come? What will it do for me?" Rules and regulations are challenged in terms of hours of work, standards of dress, and codes of conduct.

Mike Stringer provided us with an example of how his organization translates this need for casualness at Lawson Software:

It's much easier to recruit R & D people when dressed casually. Once they're here, we tell them to just dress how you need to dress. We've discovered that this may be different in other countries. The UK is a lot more formal about dress, but the barriers are breaking down there, too.

We suggest you lead Xers by helping them understand how their brusqueness impacts business. Give Xers the big picture and help them learn new behaviors. For example, explain to them how office politics can be critical to career development and can actually help them get things done. You'll need to show them the ropes; they'll get the message loud and clear. Some organizations have found, particularly those in food service, that teaching basic social skills directly is necessary to get their staff ready to interact effectively with customers and co-workers.

Many Xers want a greater piece of the organization's tangible assets. For them, money is a strong motivator primarily because it is a means to independence. And how does this concrete motivator take shape? Answer: through such opportunities as stock ownership and profit sharing. Robert Reich, Professor of Economic and Social Policy at Brandeis University and former US Secretary of Labor, noted this about the young generation in the workforce today:

For most people who are trying to decide which company to join the name of the game today is stock options . . . They're willing to forego larger salaries at bigger and better-established firms in favor of stock options in upstarts that may be worth a great deal down the road. The result: Even small, little-known enterprises can compete for top talent. In fact, startups promising high risk and huge gain are winning. (Reich, 1998, p. 128)

Leaders have told us that some of the casualness, autonomy, and balance of this generation is really quite welcomed. These behaviors become obstacles when casualness turns into rudeness, autonomy into "I'll do it my way," and balance into "I need a few days off" during a peak business period. Here, you'll need to coach the gen Xer into the performance you expect. For a summary of how leaders should coach them, refer to Box 5.2.

>> BOX 5.2   **How to coach generation Xers**

What leaders need to do	Why leaders need to do it
1 Set expectations and relate how the job fits the strategic plan.	1 Xers want the connection to the "big picture."
2 Whenever possible, involve them in deciding those actions they'll need to take.	2 They thrive on two-way discussions, in short bites. Since many are former latchkey kids and independent, they are not used to in-your-face mandates.
3 Tell them when they're doing it right.	3 They crave feedback – but in moderation, so don't overdo it.
4 Steer them when off course.	4 They want it put on the line, but not sugar-coated. This is the practical, "show me" generation.
5 Link their achievement of expectations with lateral opportunities.	5 Upward mobility is not their calling card. They want links to multiple lateral "advances."
6 Summarize what their specific performance means to *their* bottom line.	6 Performance could give them a fast-track to money. Be sure to put money where your mouth is!
7 Give honest information about organizational issues	7 Xers have low tolerance for political antics.

---

2 Start stretching boomer talent

Remember, many boomers have been working excessively long hours for years and may need to rejuvenate their energy. To avoid mid-career burnout, provide boomers with the self-actualizing experiences for which they hunger. One of the best vehicles for doing this is something academics have proudly taken for years – sabbaticals. These stimulate creativity for your organization and can even cut an organization's costs of turnover. According to Tom Peters (1996, p. 1), "Sabbaticals present a great growth opportunity for progressive organizations. Sabbaticals can provide a real boost to business innovation." Mobility leaves, another option, are

> *To avoid mid-career burnout, provide boomers with the self-actualizing experiences for which they hunger.*

popular in Minnesota state government agencies where workers can arrange to assume a position within their own, or another department, for an extended period of time to gain breadth of experiences. These don't have to be very structured or long-standing. One organization we're aware of grants its employees 12 paid days per year for community projects.

Determined to combat growing old, some baby boomers are interested in health and fitness to stay forever young. Smart leaders will recognize that motivating them could include providing fitness centers and healthy food options as an integral part of the organizational environment.

Another motivational approach for this group is to help them reassess their skills so they are adequately retooled for the future. Since they are more loyal than Xers, be sure to determine key organizational needs and help individuals figure out where they fit in. Then give them the career development opportunities they need to be successful in a new, fresh venture. It may not be a totally new career, but just a different twist of their current accountabilities.

Boomers need to be involved. This is the generation that invented participatory management and empowerment. You're likely to insult them if you leave them out of the decision-making process. Boomers value the opportunity to be engaged in charting their organization's course, whether or not they are in formal leadership roles. They've been in the workforce for many years and need to know their ideas are fully appreciated, not taken for granted.

With the talent crunch upon us, you'll also need to know how to attract baby boomers looking for their next work opportunity in a new organization. When recruiting them, don't just assess what they have done in previous jobs, but rather ask questions about the ways they've mentored others as well as the new kinds of work experiences and development opportunities they desire in their next career move. Use this information to begin making changes in your organization to attract them to it, and keep them in. You'll not only recruit more talented individuals, but you'll also establish an environment focused on staff retention. Box 5.3 (p. 87) provides a list of some of the key questions to ask baby boomers when recruiting them.

Box 5.4 summarizes the most significant strategies for tapping into boomer motivational levels to lead them most effectively.

>> BOX 5.3 **Interview questions to ask baby boomers**

- What kinds of experiences have you had in coaching others?
- What are the intangible rewards you would like to receive in your next job?
- What learning opportunities do you expect in your next career?
- What kinds of leadership inspire you?
- How would you go about coaching a peer? How about coaching someone new to the organization?
- At this point in your career, what do you most have to offer this organization?

>> BOX 5.4 **How to tap into boomer motivation**

What leaders need to do	Why leaders need to do it
1 Provide new work experiences.	1 Boomers may be close to mid-career burnout.
2 Develop sabbatical opportunities.	2 They crave rejuvenation. Help them re-energize.
3 Create mobility leaves.	3 Boomers may need to gain breadth of experiences for future career development.
4 Integrate fitness and healthy food options into your organization's culture.	4 Many want to maintain the vigor the "good life" has provided them.
5 Provide means for them to reassess their skills.	5 Many boomers are ready for a major career shift.

These strategies will help boomers retool both their professional and personal lives.

3 Start using traditionalists as sages

The wealthiest generation in American history and perhaps the world, traditionalists sometimes feel that all they have accomplished may not be held in as high esteem as it should. So one of the key leadership strategies of this generation is to be sure to recognize their talent. We have found the best way to do this is to use them as the wise sages they often are. In many of the interviews we have conducted, leaders were adamant that organizations should not bypass the important contribution traditionalists can make. Rather than always hiring outside consultants, consider using them as internal consultants to other departments or divisions. They are likely to have a rich mix of diverse skills that may be tapped into – skills and experiences that go way beyond their current assignments.

Forced retirements for most professions have become a thing of the past. This, coupled with the current labor shortage, is enough reason for any leader to consider having traditionalists become a significant part of their workforce. Probably the best reason of all, though, is that many traditionalists are motivated to work. But to retain them you'll need to use incentives, because if you don't want them another organization will, like Fort Worth-based Texas Refinery Corp. – a protective coating and specialty lubricating products firm. This organization is known for its innovative human resource practices with traditionalists. In interviewing Jerry Hopkins, President and Chief Operating Officer of Texas Refinery Corp., we discovered just how important traditionalists are to this organization. He told us,

> *Motivate traditionalists with part-time, flexible work arrangements.*

"We encourage older people. Their life experiences make them very good teachers. They have been through life's knocks and are well prepared for sales because these experiences help them connect with others. We're delighted to have them here." Pam Bell, Assistant Vice-President at Texas Refinery Corp., related some very interesting statistics to us: "Out of hundreds of active salespeople, 36 percent are in the 61- to 80-year-old category and 5 percent are in the 81+-year-old category" – a whopping 41 percent of the total workforce! Now for another statistic that will probably have you trying to find their fountain of youth, consider the ages of their top five sales people over two years in each of its domestic sales divisions – the Protective Coatings Division and the Lubricants Division. An unbelievable 55 percent of its top sales associates are between the ages of 61 and 81 (*see* Box 5.5). Jerry Hopkins summarized: "We're not a company of older salespeople; we simply welcome older salespeople."

Motivate traditionalists with part-time, flexible work arrangements. These can run the gamut from job sharing, to on-call work, to phased retirement schemes. Hire them as independent contractors who receive

---

▶▶ BOX 5.5 | **Top salespersons in the two domestic sales divisions at Texas Refinery Corp.**

Protective Coatings Division

Rank	1997 Age	1998
#1	62	63
#2	67	42
#3	58	61
#4	61	83
#5	71	67

Lubricants Division

Rank	1997 Age	1998
#1	47	45
#2	80	47
#3	47	81
#4	44	46
#5	72	44

One doesn't have to be a math whiz to determine that 55 percent (11 out of 20) of Texas Refinery Corp.'s top sales associates are between 61 and 81 years old!

commissions and benefits based on their sales. Don't rule out this generation. They are viable members of the workforce.

Motivate them also by having them become your community "arms." For traditionalists who hold leadership roles, consider providing them with opportunities to enter into executive positions "on loan" to volunteer organizations. Some of our own organizational clients have done this by providing their executives for a period of time to such community agencies as United Way. They will not only help society through these organizations, but also return to you with new vigor and creative ideas.

To make all these things happen, create an environment focused on life-long learning. To accomplish this effectively, there should be a shift not only in attitude, but also in the physical surround. We suggest you start with the physical, since this is easiest to change and can be a catalyst in altering attitudes about traditionalists. For example, traditionalists may have difficulty hearing the speakers and participants in group training programs, reading dry-erase boards and easel pages from a distance, and doing excessive amounts of team activities like outward-bound. We're not saying they can't do these things; we're cautioning leaders to take an à-la-carte approach and use selected strategies. A summary of the most meaningful learning strategies for traditionalists may be found in Box 5.6.

>> BOX 5.6   Strategies for training traditionalists

- Associating new learning with previous experiences.
- Distributing reading material for later solo review.
- Utilizing big, bold, and dark lettering on visual aids to be seen from a distance.
- Dimming the lighting minimally during video and slide presentations because a dark room is hard on the eyes and creates problems in note taking.
- Speaking in a deeper tone of voice than in typical conversations.
- Encouraging self-paced practice.
- Reducing background noise interference.

Source: Adapted from *Preparing for An Aging Workforce*

To help others understand the roles that traditionalists can and do play in organizations, establish a team of "ombudspersons" who represent the needs of late-career staff in learning programs. Have them teach and consult with others about ways to adapt the work environment. You'll also need to train organizational leaders from *all three* generations regarding how to tap most effectively into traditionalist talent, as well as how to reduce the biases prevalent about traditionalists. Box 5.7 delineates suggestions for motivating this group.

As you recruit traditionalists, focus on what's most important to them as they begin retooling their skills for the future. First of all, get out of the rut of thinking that work has to be done with full-time staff. Think of traditionalists in a contract capacity (*see* Chapter 4). This is not only good for your business, but exactly what many traditionalists are seeking. Second,

---

>> BOX 5.7   **How to motivate traditionalists**

What leaders need to do	*Why leaders need to do it*
1 Make accommodations.	1 Limitations of the aging process may affect their senses and mobility, not productivity.
2 Create flexible work arrangements.	2 Many tasks can be done anyplace, anytime.
3 Use them as consultants, internally or externally.	3 They want to be recognized for the sage advice they are capable of providing.
4 Offer top-notch retraining programs.	4 Life-long learning is their mantra.
5 Wipe out age discrimination in your organization.	5 People are successful at all ages.
6 Connect them to the community.	6 They want to help.

With talent in scarce supply, use these strategies to reconnect traditionalists to your organization's success.

---

during a job interview, focus on what the organization can learn from their experiences. Third, ask them what strategies they could use to teach others about what they have learned over the years. Don't just ask these questions because you know it's what they may want to hear. Listen and then share this with others in your organization. Box 5.8 lists sample questions you may wish to consider as you recruit traditionalists for your organization.

4   Start respecting the uniqueness of each individual

Being a leader today and in the future will require the ability to create an environment in which all generations are respected for their contributions to the organization. Take some specific lessons from organizations we know that have placed a high priority on the quality and integrity of staff interactions. Some have used a multi-disciplinary committee to develop a code of conduct or mutual respect policy and introduced it via mandatory training sessions for all staff. This credo provides a platform for giving feedback when team members display less than appropriate behaviors. At one

---

>> BOX 5.8   **Interview questions to ask traditionalists**

- How could we utilize your skills as an internal consultant in this organization?
- What skills and experiences do you have that would be useful to others? Would you be comfortable teaching these to others? If so, what would your approach be?
- What kinds of work hours are best for you?
- What types of flexibility do you need in your next job?
- What resources do you need to continue your learning?

---

organization we're aware of, a vice-president introduced the "feedback culture," which requires staff to speak directly to one another when they have concerns, "no backbiting allowed."

No matter what the generation, culture, or gender, each individual deserves to work in an organization without fear of disrespectful treatment by others. As diversity of all types has increased in the workplace, leaders must set the tone and model respect for all.

Before we profile a truly visionary leader who takes a multi-generational approach, refer to Box 5.9, which summarizes "The recognition exchange: single-generational for multi-generational focus."

>> BOX 5.9   **The recognition exchange: single-generational for multi-generational focus**

Stop	Start
1 Squeezing the motivation out of generation Xers.	1 Tapping into Xers' independence and flexibility.
2 Stagnating the careers of baby boomers.	2 Stretching boomer talent.
3 Cutting off traditionalists from pivotal organizational activities.	3 Using traditionalists as sages.
4 Thinking everyone wants what you want.	4 Respecting the uniqueness of each individual.

An insightful leader with a multi-generational focus

Tim Fliss

Vice-President, Human Resources, Schneider Corporation

Meet Tim Fliss, who is a vice-president at Schneider Corporation, the mega-transportation and logistics firm with 20 000 associates (the word they use for "employees"), located in Green Bay, Wisconsin. By striving to diversify their workforce, attract the best associates, and retain the talent they work so hard to develop, this organization has successfully created a multi-generational focus. Listen to how Tim has led this effort with his very talented human resource team at the helm.

Q *How do you attract the best talent to Schneider?*

A We do this in three ways. First of all, we create challenging work for our associates. Second, Schneider Corporation presents a variety of career growth opportunities. And third, we address work–life perspectives by creating an environment that recognizes and supports the need for flexible work options – a very simple concept that is just one more thing that we can do to be the employer of choice. This allows us to bring the best associates here and retain them. What this incorporates is a variety of options that allow our associates to choose flexible schedules to balance work and home. We have found that this is a particularly useful strategy for the different generations in our own workforce today. For example, compared to five to ten years ago when no one was on a flexible schedule, approximately 10 out of 60 associates in our own human resource team use the work–life options we offer them.

Q *What are some of the more successful strategies you've used with generation Xers?*

A We have found it extremely important to use these strategies with both our non-manager *and* manager associates. Let's take one of our more unique examples: managers who want work–life options. We encourage part-time managers here at Schneider. We've found this strategy particularly successful for the generation X managers out there. We know that a significant reason many of them apply to Schneider is because we note the availability of flexible scheduling in the ad. One manager we recently hired with an engineering degree and an MBA told us that she had so many job offers that the primary reason for taking this job was our tailor-made work–life option. Another generation X manager related to us that it was our compressed work week that was most attractive to her.

▶

➤ Another strategy we've been playing with is late start-times for associates in the Midwest, handling our West Coast business. This is perfect because we need people starting and working later in the Midwest to accommodate the earlier time zone on the West Coast.

We have also found this generation to respond more than any other to a flexible arrangement of work locations. We had to get out of the mindset of a one work-site location. To do this, Schneider offers leaders jobs in one location with a promise for a change in 18 months to a customer site. This is particularly useful for generation X leaders who want variety in their jobs. And some of this variety can come from choice of location. Schneider Corporation also provides a Frontline Leadership Development Program that addresses the leadership needs of first-time managers, many of whom are generation Xers.

In general, Schneider Corporation and our associates are very pleased with the results of part-time opportunities, compressed work weeks, flex start-times, and remote reporting. We still have work to do here from two perspectives. First, as change agents, our associates in the Human Resource Department shouldn't underestimate the resistance to change accompanying these efforts. Second, we try to help leaders understand that we're talking about evolutionary kinds of things that need to grow and nurture, *not* revolutionary stuff.

Q *What about strategies for baby boomers?*

A This has been a tough one for us because sometimes we've taken for granted the tremendous efforts they've made to this organization. Because there's been so much competition for good jobs, they've worked hard. Due to their hard work, the "bar" has been raised and, subsequently, we have raised our own expectations of them. We've paused, looked at what they need *and* what Schneider needs, and designed a state-of-the-art leadership development process. While the audience is certainly all three generations, this program is something that the baby boomer leaders, in particular, tell us they have needed for a long time. We have an intensive four-day residential development program called the Leadership Forum, which targets mid-to-senior level leaders. Here we do everything from 360° feedback, simulations, case studies, and formal and informal team-building activities – all designed to give leaders a process for looking at themselves, their roles at Schneider, and what they personally need to do to plan strategically for their *own* leadership development. And we know they're using what they've learned because they not only tell us continuously, but more importantly, they're applying it. We see it in meetings, performance appraisals, and even in some of the strategic planning they do.

Q *What about strategies for the traditionalists?*

A We have found one very interesting strategy that works for us. Consider that some of our drivers are either retired military personnel or empty nesters. Since we're having a hard time finding good driver associates, we've tapped into this group with the concept of husband–wife team drivers. Believe it or not, this is working for us.

Q *Many generation X individuals prefer to be individual contributors, not leaders with a formal management title. What do you do to attract generation X individuals to new leadership roles?*

A At Schneider Corporation, we create opportunities with sizzle! In the past, we couldn't attract them to our small city in the upper Midwest. Now we're attracting the cream of the crop. We put these individuals, most of whom are generation Xers, on rotational assignments in key parts of the business. The sizzle comes in as we integrate some of what they love, like technology, into these assignments. We make a real concerted effort to do this. We also provide in these assignments lots of project-type work and opportunities to have a significant impact on the business. This is something we believe we *have* to do because we're having difficulty finding the best talent. With the previous generation, baby boomers, a leadership career was what many of them wanted and they were motivated to move up the career ladder. We really didn't have to do much to attract them to this. We now have to do more with generation Xers. With these new opportunities, we're having fantastic success; we have tripled the number of people in this program from 1998 to 1999.

Q *What's next for Schneider Corporation with the multi-generational focus?*

A We know that we don't have enough points of entry for young grads. What our very talented human resource team is trying to do is determine how we can best position ourselves with these individuals. Part of the strategic planning process for our human resources team has been sometimes to create and expand these points of entry.

Changing our selection process is another "next" for us. In our strategic planning process, we have come up with 22 very specific action items aimed at helping us attract, develop, and retain talent. We know that generation X has a "what can you do for me" philosophy. This isn't bad, just different from what we've been used to. We need to address this in our recruiting process, which has been a data-driven, extract-as-much-as-possible, approach. We can't just ask at the *end* of the interview, "By the way, do you have any questions?" We're going to focus on listening to them more during the interview. We want to really get to know them. And that can be as simple as not scribbling copious notes while they're talking. We will ask them if they have

➤

► any special personal needs we need to be aware of that can "sell" them on the job. And you've got to be honest with them. If you feel good about how the interview went, then it's really OK to tell them that. We ask them what variables will be most important in their decision-making process and then address this with the interviewing team. One other important question to ask them is, "If you have two offers, what would weigh most heavily on your decision?" Then, we do everything possible to address this question. This is just a beginning at Schneider and we think integrating these new perspectives is a great place to go!

REFERENCES

Coopers & Lybrand (1997) *Coopers & Lybrand International Student Survey Summary Findings Report.*

Johnson, B. (1998) "Job crunch can be eased through better IT management," *StarTribune,* 9 November, D3.

Newman, K. S. (1993) *Declining Fortunes: The Withering of the American Dream.* New York: Basic Books.

Peters, T. (1996) "Think sabbaticals," *Fast Forward,* October, 1–3.

Preparing for An Aging Workforce (1998) Washington, DC: American Association of Retired Persons (AARP).

Reich, R. B. (1998) "The company of the future," *Fast Company,* Issue 19, 124–150.

Sterling, W. and Waite, S. (1998) *Boomernomics.* New York: The Ballantine Publishing Group.

THE TEAM EXCHANGE

Siloed and local for fluid and geographically dispersed

R ichard Fogel is the recently hired CEO of an engineering consulting firm. As he sits in his office, looking at the urban landscape outside, he ponders a critical question: how can he get the teams the firm has put in place over the last five-year period to function more effectively? At present, the firm is organized by functional departments: electrical, structural, mechanical, and chemical engineering. While the department teams work reasonably well within themselves, turf protection and inter-unit competition have clearly resulted in significant inefficiencies. Communication is guarded as departments focus on their own best interests rather than the company strategic goals. Projects manage to get completed via the "pass off" method, with each department completing its portion and passing it to the next, often with minimal coordination. While the firm has clearly taken strides to build more teamwork, it seems to Richard the model being utilized is limited.

Richard is considering breaking down the team model by making two changes: first, creating an overlay of cross-functional teams to work on specific organizational issues, i.e. continuous improvement initiatives; second, building a matrix structure through which engineers would come out of their functional structures to work on cross-functional project teams, maintaining their home base in their functions. He reasons that this approach would allow the functional staff to keep their like-type groupings and at the same time would force more collaborative project effort. He begins to sketch his plan by adding dotted lines to the current organizational chart, showing how staff members would be "matrixed out" to team assignments.

Sound like a great plan? Maybe not. While Richard is exploring some popular team development routes, he may not be going far enough to make truly effective change. If his goals are to increase flexibility of staff and break down the silos of separate, functional reporting structures having specialized roles, he may still be one step behind in his thinking. Here's why.

COMMON PROBLEMS IN TRADITIONAL TEAM BUILDING

While many team-building approaches currently used in organizations have been successful in creating cohesion and collaborative relationships, they still fall short in producing the optimal levels of flexibility needed in today's high-speed organizations. Cross-functional team approaches, which assemble members from multiple departments to work on projects, can re-create the same problems inherent in functional organizational structures, particularly if the team compositions are permanent. As the teams stabilize and coalesce, they may become turf-protected and competitive with one another in much the same way departments and divisions do in a "siloed" structure. By breaking down one set of walls and re-designing the configuration, another set of walls is potentially installed.

Symptoms of excessive competition and turf protection begin with secretive behavior and the accompanying guarded communication. Teams, as well as individuals, withhold what they know as they begin to see information as an important power-building tool. They share only what they must and hoard as much as they can get by with. Inter-team behavior, when competition is fueled, can result in divisiveness – deliberate attempts by teams to disrupt other teams' goal attainments. These behaviors become more pronounced when leaders hand out rewards based on individual or team-based goal attainment alone with no recognition for collaborative efforts toward the organization's strategic goals.

Rosabeth Moss Kanter in *When Giants Learn to Dance* (1989) describes infighting among scientists in one governmental organization that accelerated to the point that they tampered with one another's experiments, throwing away research materials and slowing publication of results. When internal competition between groups gets out of control, the focus is diverted from performance and innovation, Kanter concludes. More attention is directed toward beating the competitors than getting the job done.

Another common problem teams may face is not having an adequate skill mix within the competencies of given team members. When membership is selected across functional areas, sometimes representatives are chosen based on faulty criteria: who has time to fill the assignment, who needs something to do, or simply whose turn it might be. This does not guarantee members will have the best qualifications for the task at hand.

Additionally, the rapid increase in cross-functional teaming has over-loaded many staff persons, particularly those with specialized skills, limiting their ability to participate effectively in the teams to which they are assigned.

Yet another problem with cross-functional teams is the issue of perfor-mance management. Many team leaders within these structures report their lack of position authority makes it difficult to deal with team member performance problems. In a typical matrix structure, cross-functional teams are formed but the reporting relationship remains to the functional man-ager who does the performance appraisal. Given that cross-functional teams typically involve as many as ten members, the communication chal-lenge of working through potentially ten different functional managers can be overwhelming. And, it can slow down decision making signifi-cantly if team members have to go back through their departments to get approval.

To reduce the problems described, a leader who wants to build teams should stop utilizing ineffective team-building strategies that fuel the prob-lems we've just described, adopting, instead, a new set of team development approaches. We call this "The team exchange: siloed and local for fluid and geographically dispersed."

STOP DOING THESE THINGS

1 Stop growing silos

Silos are produced when leaders design organizations comprised of fixed, linear units with specialized roles. There are three types of linear structures that we recommend leaders begin to reduce in their organizations. First, the classic functional structure promotes and reinforces professional identities (e.g. marketing, finance, production, customer ser-vice), but sets up barriers as staff within the functions become focused on only part of the whole work process and flow. This segmented view can lead to decisions that disrupt the work of other functional

> *A narrow field of vision yields wasted time, wasted effort, and multiple inefficiencies.*

units when their needs are not taken into account. A narrow field of vision yields wasted time, wasted effort, and multiple inefficiencies.

We also know from the creativity literature that when people try to solve problems in an isolated fashion without considering the views of multiple stakeholders, innovation decreases. Silos in functional structures reduce the probability of collecting diverse perspectives and, therefore, limit the potential for innovation when creativity is paramount to this just-in-time, knowledge-based world. The bottom line? Functional silos inhibit multi-disciplinary involvement which, in turn, leads to reduced organizational effectiveness.

Another siloed organizational form is the divisional structure, made up of relatively autonomous divisions according to a product line or geographic area. The divisional structure essentially re-creates the functional form under each division, but may promote more cross-fertilization at the top as leaders from multiple functions manage their operations. Yet, it is fraught with the same problems inherent in the functional model: too much inefficiency, slow response time, and lack of multi-disciplinary problem solving and innovation.

The third type of organizational structure, which promotes silos, is the matrix organization. Initiated in the aerospace industry in the 1960s, it reached its height in the late 1970s and early 1980s, and still runs rampant in many organizations today. Individuals still report up the ladder, but they also have a dotted-line relationship to someone else, typically a project team leader or multi-disciplinary unit manager. For example, in one ambulatory care clinic of a hospital in Manhattan, nurses report directly to the nursing manager, lab technologists to the laboratory manager, and staff physicians to the medical director. But, they have a dotted-line relationship to the administrator of the ambulatory care clinic. What does this mean? In practical terms, the functional leaders (e.g. the nursing manager) have the final say on the hiring, firing, and performance appraisals. The clinic administrator may give input, sometimes quite actively, but it's the direct line leader who has the final say. While certainly an improvement over the functional structure because it provides for cross-fertilization of ideas, the matrix essentially combines two sets of hierarchy and creates possible confusion as staff members struggle with two or more leaders they must report to.

While all these models have merit in some situations, leaders must stop automatically growing them. They do not promote the flexibility, efficiency, and innovation that organizations need to be effective. Staff members become constrained by confinement to their functional units. Their interactions, and potential contributions to the organization, are constricted compared to their potential if they were released to work more fluidly throughout the organization.

2 Stop creating so many permanent, ongoing teams

As you develop teams, no matter what organizational design you use, stop thinking of their membership and leadership as permanent. Organizational agility requires less use of stable structures, which put a clamp on staff resources, limiting flexibility. Once team members are assigned to a permanent team, a leader creates the same conditions inherent in siloed organizations. Walls go up, and inter-team competition and self-focus may begin to brew. Team members can't help but develop loyalty to their long-term relationships among one another. The commitment must lie with the organization's values and goals, not to a sub-group alone. Team members need to know how they contribute to the organization's product or service and, ultimately, to its vision.

3 Stop thinking narrowly and locally about team membership

Traditional team-building efforts begin by searching for team membership within a given organization and/or at a specific physical site. Why narrow the search, given the potent technological linkages available? As we learned through our interviews with stellar global team leaders, membership can potentially be crafted across geographical boundaries once the technology is in place. Leaders must stop thinking about staff resources as if they exist within the confines of buildings and physical space.

> *Leaders must stop thinking about staff resources as if they exist within the confines of buildings and physical space.*

4 Stop putting team leaders in power binds

By creating cross-functional, matrixed team models that result in team members reporting to team leaders who are not responsible for their performance management, the leaders suffer from lack of formal authority. They are forced to work around troublesome team members, particularly when informal feedback is not effective. Rendered powerless by lack of management support and clout, their leadership effectiveness is often compromised when they have to contend with stressful group dynamics without the benefit of formal authority. They run the risk that productive team members may lose their motivation because non-productive team members' disruptive behavior continues without adequate intervention.

5 Stop maintaining teams that have out-lived their usefulness

Many teams are established because a specific need arises, but when their mission is accomplished they struggle to find a purpose in life. Wasting time and effort, they drastically lose productivity when leaders do not disband them. When team structures are designed as permanent, it becomes difficult to find a place in the organization for team members, once a team is no longer needed. Often, we find, bogus activities are assigned to the team, seemingly to mark time until, hopefully, something more valuable can be found for the team to do.

6 Stop fabricating reward systems that fuel competition

By neglecting to align rewards to team and organizational goal attainment, leaders sabotage their own efforts at building collaboration. Asking staff members to collaborate when they know their rewards will be based on individual accomplishments breeds individualistic thinking and its accompanying self-focused behavior. Team members who are aware their individual performance appraisals will be based on their personal talents and individual performance may have difficulty investing fully in collaborative behaviors – sharing information, teaching others, compromising – when it may cause others to out-pace them at review time.

START DOING THESE THINGS

As you build teams, remember to assess your approach for its power to break down competition, maximize utilization of staff resources, and create conditions for effective team leadership to thrive. Start doing these things to grow winning teams, positioned to help your organization compete in the new millennium.

1 Start creating more virtual teams, spanning geographical boundaries

Virtual teams, by definition, are comprised of members who exist in disparate locations but are interconnected through technology. Team members communicate more frequently through e-mail, videoconferencing, or teleconferencing, as well as groupware – software that facilitates on-line problem solving and ideation. Virtual teaming allows leaders to create teams of people from anywhere in the world and might include customers, vendors, or even world-renowned experts in a given field. Team members can be selected from across different time zones to be productive over multiple work periods. Some staff may be on-site, others working from home, yet others in remote locations. Virtual teams work particularly well for global organizations but can also be beneficial to smaller ones operating from a single location, especially when staff members are often on the road or at job sites. The possibilities are endless.

Microsoft's success in many industries is directly related to the company's ability to network with software developers within their supplier organizations. Microsoft facilitates communication with its customers and acquires feedback prior to releasing final versions of its productions through virtual teams of suppliers and Microsoft staff (Townsend, DeMarie, and Hendrickson, 1998).

Mike Barnoski, President of ABB CE Nuclear Power in Windsor, Connecticut, said, "Virtual work has improved our ability to manage projects in Korea from the US. Electronic media has made it easier to create a team environment. It has always been a struggle to create dialogue." CEO Karl Stauber of Northwest Area Foundation, talked about leadership in the virtual arena, noting "Proximity should not be the critical variable of leadership."

2 Start developing a technological infrastructure to support high-performance virtual team development

To make virtual teams perform effectively, put in place as much technology as you can. While e-mail, videoconferencing, and teleconferencing are standard fare, take the leap to the next dimension of virtual team building – technological tools.

Begin with collaborative software systems, sometimes called groupware.

Typically, these software systems allow team members jointly to author documents and presentations, develop data bases and spreadsheets, as well as combine scheduling and electronic messaging. Work may be done independently and shared via the software or done at the same time, on-line.

Another type of collaborative software is called group decision support systems. These are designed to create an on-line environment for group problem solving, including brainstorming and categorization of ideas, as well as polling of team members to prioritize alternatives. One of the advantages of these systems is that they allow for anonymity as ideation is conducted, reducing the impact of status differences within a group as team members work together.

Next, prepare for the addition of Desktop Videoconferencing Systems (DVCSs). While virtual teams can exist with simple e-mail and telephones, they flourish when face-to-face interaction is simulated through DVCS. DVCS makes videoconferencing convenient by allowing team members to hold meetings at their PCs, as the screen splits to reveal visual images of each team member. A small camera is typically mounted on top of each team member's computer monitor to provide the video feed to the system, while an earpiece or speakerphone provides audio input. Groups of up to 16 members can conference on most systems and may allow for conferencing with others tapping in from a more traditional teleconferencing site. DVCS allows team members to share information, work on documents and problem solve while conferencing. Box 6.1 provides a list of popular collaborative software and desktop videoconferencing systems.

Soon, these technologies may sprint ahead further, allowing problem-solving team members to put their heads together with some of the best minds in the world, the ultimate extended team membership! TechOptimizer is an application designed by Invention Machine Corporation that allows teams to get the smarts of Leonardo da Vinci, Thomas Edison, and the Wright Brothers all rolled into one. The team enters a problem into the query field and the software searches a data base from other disciplines to find solutions to similar problems. In a study comparing the number of solutions to a problem generated by two established teams, the one using TechOptimizer was found to generate twice as many ideas within one hour (Farnady, 1998).

Now, build your technological infrastructure further via the Internet and intranet. By establishing their own Web sites, virtual teams can keep other organizational members, customers, and vendors aware of their

---

>> BOX 6.1 **Collaborative support systems and desktop videoconferencing resources**

Collaborative support systems

- Lotus Notes
- TeamFlow, CFM, Inc.
- Groupwise, Novell
- Collabra Share, Netscape
- FirstClass 3.0, First Arc
- Microsoft Exchange
- Groupware Solutions, Oracle
- TeamTalk 2.0, Trax Softworks
- eRoom 3.0, instinctiv<u>e</u>

Desktop videoconferencing resources

- Intel ProShare Conferencing System 200
- PictureTel Live 200p
- CorelVIDEO, CorelCAM
- VCON Armada Escrot 50
- Apple QuickTime Conferencing ISDN Kit
- Creative Labs Sharevision PC3000

Ask your information systems department staff or consultant to assist you in choosing the best resources for your needs.

---

activities. In addition, teams can store documents and monitor ongoing project activity. The Internet provides access to limitless information as team members research new ideas or find out what others in similar industries might be doing that is relevant to the team's work.

The possibilities of the virtual workplace are endless. Robert Stevens, President and CEO of Ridgeview Medical Center, analyzes the power of the virtual workplace to improve the way we work:

> *The workplace of the future will be less around bricks, mortar, and a central location. We're looking at taking all our transcriptionists and putting them in their homes. Mayo Clinic is well ahead of the game with telemedicine, linking practitioners and patients. It's as though the physician and patient are in the same room; in fact it's better because the camera documentation will actually magnify better than individual eyesight.*

Technology has dramatically changed from the days of unfriendly systems that took way too long to master. Mike Peterson, Senior Vice-President of Merchandise Planning and Merchandise Presentation at The Department Store Division of Dayton-Hudson Corporation, told us:

In the past, everything was on the mainframe – greenscreen, cryptic commands, not intuitive – which took a year to learn. Now, we're building "GUI" (Graphic User Interface – pronounced "gooey") applications. It's all point and click – highly intuitive. While people were once afraid to push the enter key, now they're not because you can always get back to your original spot. Systems are also more integrated. Information goes into one system and the data feed off each other, instead of having to enter the same information in multiple systems with many chances for error.

3 Start building virtual team member and team leader capability

> **Virtual team members must learn how to communicate effectively without being physically present, utilizing technology to get their message across.**

Virtual team members will need new sets of skills to function successfully in a new type of work setting. Ensure they get formal training on how to communicate in a virtual environment. Virtual team members must learn how to communicate effectively without being physically present, utilizing technology to get their message across. Ensure they get formal training on how to communicate in a virtual environment.

Given the fluidity of virtual teams, members will need to build relationships and assimilate quickly. Spanning the boundaries of time and space, these teams will require members who can work across cultures adeptly. Additionally, when they communicate with less visual interface, status differences tend to be downplayed, changing the traditional social structure (*see* Chapter 8 on the "workplace exchange"). Therefore, title alone will not give a team member clout. In the world of virtual teaming, members will be known more for the quality of their ideas and their ability to influence others and meet their commitments.

By reducing physical limitations as a criterion for team structuring, individual team members can be selected primarily for their skills. In other words, team members must build a reputation for their competencies when functional representation is not the primary selection factor. Technical training will have to be high-powered and cutting edge to assist members in "adding value" to the teams in which they engage. Box 6.2 provides a summary of desirable virtual team member skill sets.

Team leaders, on the other hand, will need some additional competencies. Virtual team building will require the ability to coach individuals

---

>> BOX 6.2 **Virtual team member skills**

1 Proficiency with technical tools:
- e-mail;
- collaborative software systems;
- Internet;
- intranet;
- desktop videoconferencing systems;
- non-desktop videoconferencing systems;
- teleconferencing.

2 Ability to form team relationships effectively:
- entering new teams via introduction of self, asking questions to help the team get organized, and showing interest in others;
- quickly ascertaining other team members' preferred work styles and adapting their own accordingly.

3 Ability to communicate in a virtual environment:
- command of written communication skills for utilization via e-mail and collaborative software systems;
- communicating effectively via videoconferencing for team meetings;
- making formal presentations through videoconferencing.

4 Ability to access, analyze, and manage data.

5 Ability to communicate across cultures:
- awareness of cultural differences among team members;
- adjusting communication approach based on those differences, when appropriate.

6 Basic teamwork skills:
- managing differences;
- participating effectively in group problem solving;
- cooperating with others;
- setting goals.

Use this list of desired skills to develop training programs and to select team members for various projects.

---

and facilitate group meetings on-line. While many of the interpersonal skills will remain the same, team leaders must develop some specialized virtual leadership capabilities. Box 6.3 is a summary of desirable virtual

---

>> BOX 6.3 **Virtual team leader skills**

1 Proficiency with technical tools:
- e-mail;
- collaborative software systems;
- Internet;
- intranet;
- desktop videoconferencing systems;
- non-desktop videoconferencing systems;
- teleconferencing.

2 Ability to facilitate meetings:
- face-to-face meetings;
- on-line meetings;
- videoconferencing.

3 Ability to coach team members, on-line and face-to-face:
- giving work direction;
- giving performance feedback;
- motivating and encouraging.

4 Ability to align team initiatives with organizational needs:
- providing linkage from team to organization;
- serving as advocate from team to organization;
- interpreting organizational initiatives to team.

5 Ability to communicate in a virtual environment:
- sending and receiving messages via technology;
- communicating persuasively;
- explaining change effectively.

6 Ability to access, analyze, and manage data.

7 Ability to communicate across cultures:
- awareness of cultural differences among team members;
- adjusting communication approach based on those differences, when appropriate.

Use this list of desired skills to develop training programs and to select team leaders for various projects.

---

team leader skill sets and Box 6.4 gives guidelines for leading virtual teams.

>> BOX 6.4   **Guidelines for leading virtual teams**

- Early in the process, gather face-to-face and go through a series of team-development activities.
- Post pictures of team members on-line or close to your desk.
- Create a team Web site or bulletin board.
- Post team goals on the Web site or at each team member's work station.
- Communicate more often than you might if the team were on-site.
- Check in periodically and systematically with each team member and the team as a whole to monitor progress.
- Don't neglect ongoing personal communication. Have periodic face-to-face meetings with team members, individually and as a group.

Source: Adapted from Thuermer, 1996

---

4 Start thinking of teams as "migrating"

At Barr Engineering, a consulting firm in Minneapolis, a fluid approach to teams is the norm. When a project is acquired, a team leader is selected from among the senior staff and is responsible for assembling the team membership by soliciting participation. Team leaders are typically selected by the client. Staff members can choose to participate on the team or not, depending on their workloads. On the other hand, staff members are less likely to be chosen for team membership if they have not developed a reputation for a strong, desirable skill set. This interplay is what Barr Engineering refers to as a "free enterprise" system. Once the project work is complete, the team is disbanded and members focus on their other projects with other teams. Staff members chronically short of project assignments are provided feedback on the issues that seem to be causing the situation. "Often any problem can be corrected through additional training or self-awareness. Occasionally, the staff member realizes that they are not well suited to the Barr value system and moves on," notes Allan Gebhard, President of Barr Engineering. In this fluid, "migrating" model, staff are not rigidly assigned to a functional unit. They work for themselves, so to speak.

This model of organizational design is essentially "de-organized" in that it lends itself to leaders thinking of staff as one big pool from which to draw. In fact, that's what the President of the Danish hearing aid manufacturer, Oticon, does. After years of trying to turn the company around using strategic marketing techniques and cost-cutting methods, he decided to turn the company into one giant virtual team. By tearing down walls, cutting secretarial positions, and eliminating job descriptions and specialties, the President created a totally project-directed entity in which staff invent the work that needs to be done, then physically arrange themselves in ways to get the work done (Peters, 1994).

So think of your workforce as one large talent pool. As projects end, staff and leaders can disband and shift to other projects. Unleash your staff from the binds of structure and build a fluid system.

5 Start combining core and non-core staff (and customers) in creative compositions

As we discussed in Chapter 4, non-core staff should be treated as critical members of the organization. Ensure they are an integral part of each team and that team activities accommodate their needs. In some cases, you might even consider creating an entire team of non-core staff, writing into their performance agreements that team participation is a critical element of the work they deliver to your organization. Why not assign a non-core staff person as the team leader if their skills are best suited for the job?

> *Ensure the non-core staff are an integral part of each team and that team activities accommodate their needs.*

Consider adding internal or external customers to the team composition. In one health care organization with which we consult, the Materials Management Division puts members from the Accounts Payable Department on their operational teams to ensure close collaboration and efficiency. Also, key vendors office within the Materials Management Division and serve on teams as well. In many of our client organizations, customers have taken on more active roles in the teams who serve them.

6 Start designing reward systems that fuel collaboration

Begin by making sure each team has a set of specific, measurable goals. The trick here will be to establish measures that can answer the question, "How will we know these goals have been attained? What evidence can we produce?" Then ensure a tracking system is in place for collecting information about team progress. Next, examine the performance appraisal tools your organization utilizes. Make sure to add criteria related to staff members' team skills and their contributions to team performance. Discard evaluation procedures that put team members in competition with one another, i.e. systems that rank team members or make comparisons between them. Be certain the evaluation mechanism provides input from other team members, managers, and customers for each evaluation.

The review should include an assessment of how well the team met its given goals. It should also include a summary of the team members' self-evaluation of their own contributions to the team along with how others view their performance. We have found that all team members typically share in the same evaluation on the team measures which are factored into those used for assessment of individual contribution to the team. For example, a team may receive an overall evaluation of 4 on a 5-point scale for its goal attainment, while the individual may receive an evaluation of 5 for his or her contributions. The team member's overall rating, given the weighting of each number is the same, would be a 4.5. This puts muscle behind the fact that both the individual and the team are critical to organizational success.

With the advent of virtual teams, an interesting phenomenon has been cited. As new technology creates a sense of shared work and purpose, merging ideas and document generation in an on-line environment, it may be increasingly difficult to differentiate an individual's work from that of the team (Mankin, Cohen, and Bikson, 1996). You may find as you develop your organization's virtual teaming capability that the value of individual performance reviews may be limited.

Besides formal rewards, consider more informal team rewards. The typical pizza lunches, public recognition events, and loud applause become a bit more tricky when the teams you want to say "thank you" to are geographically dispersed. While it may be no problem to show appreciation via e-mail or videoconference, the hands-on rewards will require more imagination. Many virtual team leaders with whom we talked hosted periodic face-to-face meetings with their team members, often at rotating locations, to ensure they had the opportunity to recognize them live. In between those events, they had lunch delivered to team members individually at their sites; sent balloons, candy, flowers; or used on-line greeting cards. (Try www.bluemountain.com for free greeting cards.)

Box 6.5 summarizes "The team exchange: siloed and local for fluid and geographically dispersed." Use it as a guideline as you develop teams in your organization.

>> BOX 6.5 **The team exchange: siloed and local for fluid and geographically dispersed**

Stop	Start
1 Growing silos.	**1** Creating more virtual teams, spanning geographic boundaries.
2 Creating so many permanent, ongoing teams.	**2** Developing a technological infrastructure to support high-performance virtual team development.
3 Thinking narrowly and locally about team membership.	**3** Building virtual team member and team leader capability.
4 Putting team leaders in power binds.	**4** Thinking of teams as "migrating."
5 Maintaining teams that have outlived their usefulness.	**5** Combining core and non-core staff (and customers) in creative compositions.
6 Fabricating reward systems that fuel competition.	**6** Designing reward systems that fuel collaboration.

LEADER PROFILE

A stellar virtual team builder

Susan Lund, Ph.D.,
Senior Director of Staff Operations,
Oracle Corporation

Dr Susan Lund is Senior Director of Staff Operations for Oracle Corporation, the second largest software company in the world, next to Microsoft. Oracle specializes in data bases with two product lines: a generic data base and applications, specialized for specific industries such as human resources, financial services, and manufacturing. In addition to the product lines, Oracle provides consulting services, product support, and education. Susan's role is within the education business line, managing the Office of Customer Loyalty and overseeing staff for the education program center. She manages multiple virtual teams, most consisting of staff who do not report directly to her, as well as team members located throughout North and South America.

Here are her perspectives on what it takes to make a virtual team work effectively:

Q *What characteristics do you look for in virtual team members?*

A Excellent communication skills. Virtual team members may never meet some of their team members, yet they have to communicate effectively. Persuasive communication is very important since some of the initiatives cross-departmental teams work on may not be of prime priority to all team members. Virtual team members have to be clear communicators and document, then follow-up, completing the feedback loop. Lots of things can potentially slip through the cracks in virtual teams. The ability to be a self-starter and take initiative is important.

Q *How do you go about building a virtual team?*

A I have people meet face-to-face at least once so team members are more than just a voice on the phone to one another. The second best method is through videoconferencing. Relationships end up being real important. Then, I establish clear priorities and communicate them over and over again. When working with departments and staff not reporting to me, I try to make it easy for everyone to participate. I volunteer to do the agenda, set up the meeting logistics, and send out information.

Q *What obstacles to virtual team building have you encountered?*

A With the speed at which many staff members are working, there is sometimes an unwillingness to invest in the relationship building – dinner together, a team-building retreat. I think it is hard to really invest in a team when you are receiving e-mail from people you don't know. In a virtual team environment, you have to do everything consciously. You don't find out about things by running into people in the hallway. No one is there to spontaneously remind you of something. You can't get away with everything. The problems become glaring.

Q *How do you reward your virtual teams?*

A I essentially do the same thing I would with any type of team: use individual and group rewards. I send flowers to team members' homes, give movie and dinner tickets, send e-mail notes both to the team member and their manager. What is different, though, is that I do it more often.

115

Q *How do you go about ending a virtual team?*

A To close out, I do three things. First, I write a note to the team to say the task has been completed and the team is disbanding. Second, I write a note to the organization indicating the job is done, who the team was, and who assisted the team. Third, I do something nice for the team members.

Q *What additional thoughts do you have about virtual teams?*

A The key to leading virtual teams is over-communication. In an influence environment, when all team members don't report directly to you, get buy-in by staying in touch with each team member's manager. Include those managers in the final celebration. Otherwise, the danger is too much team member independence and apathy about projects they have deemed low priority. Finally, you can't forget you are still dealing with humans. Remember the common courtesies, even though you are communicating via technology.

REFERENCES

Farnady, K. (1998) "Brainbase," *Wired*, June, 6.06, 7.

Kanter, R. (1989) *When Giants Learn to Dance*. New York: Simon & Schuster.

Mankin, D., Cohen, S., and Bikson, T. (1996) *Teams and Technology: Fulfilling the Promise of the New Organization*. Boston: Harvard Business School Press.

Peters, T. (1994) *The Tom Peters Seminar: Crazy Times Call for Crazy Organizations*. New York: Vintage Books.

Thuermer, K. (1996) "Here, There, and Everywhere," *Human Resource Executive*, 10 (12), 43–5.

Townsend, A., DeMarie, S., and Hendrickson, A. (1998) "Virtual teams: Technology and the workplace of the future," *Academy of Management Executive*, 12 (3), 17–29.

THE DEVELOPMENT EXCHANGE

Excessive team building for individual maverick appreciation

J im Johnson is described by managers and peers alike as the brightest, most innovative engineer his medium-sized medical device company has ever employed. When confronted with a tough technical problem, his solutions are not only effective, but unique, setting apart the company's product line from others in the field. No one quite understands how his mind works; it seems as if he takes in information, then sits in silence as ideas incubate for several minutes, even hours, until brilliant, atypical solutions emerge. While his technical contributions to the company are stellar, some would say irreplaceable, Jim presents significant challenges to his team members and his manager. Simply stated, he is bull-headed. Jim rarely listens to others' points of view, often treating them as if they have nothing of value to contribute. He does not tolerate ineptness very gracefully. Jim is stubborn, independent and only selectively helps others. Rebellious toward authority, he often side-steps policies he views as unnecessary and does not take direction readily from his manager, Suzanne Wu. Yet Jim is intensely passionate about his work and cares deeply that the product he designs is created with the highest quality standards in mind. His work is his passion, his obsession.

Suzanne continually places Jim on project teams and he, in turn, manages to show intolerance for the group process. Suzanne has sent him to team-member effectiveness training and given him some individual feedback, although she has been reluctant to antagonize him since his technical skills and quality orientation are immensely valuable. While these interventions produce some softening of Jim's behavior, eventually he reverts to full-strength maverick iconoclasm. In spite of his clashes with those staff members who do not hold his views or are not strong problem solvers, Jim does have good relationships with two of his peers who are also brilliant technicians and match his *modus operandi*.

THE CHALLENGE AND OPPORTUNITY
MAVERICKS PRESENT

Jim is characteristic of the renegade type we call the "maverick." Difficult to corral and tame, mavericks relish their freedom and buck the notion of others telling them what to do, unless the direction comes from someone they highly respect. Because their tendency is to pull away from the pack, they often resist conforming to group norms and perform best when working on their own or with others of like mind. They are bright and imaginative, typically seeing situations with a much different twist than others and may have difficulty articulating their thought process. Yet, they are invaluable in their problem-solving capability and ability to muster up innovative solutions to difficult problems. Box 7.1 provides a list of maverick-like characteristics to help you identify those you work with who fit the profile.

➤➤ BOX 7.1   **Maverick-like characteristics**

zealous	good problem solver
passionate	relentless
forceful	impatient
tenacious	controversial
unconventional	visionary
intolerant	intuitive
risk taking	curious
fluent in ideation	energetic

During the last decade of organizational life, when teams have sprung up about as fast as Minnesota mosquitoes multiply in the summertime, mavericks have suffered from leader's attempts to mold them into all-purpose team players. It seems as if leaders have assumed that every staff person must be molded into a team member *par excellence*, leaving little room for individuality to have its place. We know, however, that better decisions are made in groups *except* when the creativity or expertise of an individual member far exceeds that of other team members. Under those conditions, the maverick's often quirky way of thinking is forced to conform to group norms and the benefits of their brain power are rarely brought to fruition. In the process, the frustration, even anger, of being pushed to adapt, stifles the maverick's effectiveness.

So, the challenge presented to leaders here is paradoxical. How can they capture the talent of those renegade mavericks while still maximizing the benefits of team building? We're not saying mavericks can't perform well in teams. We are suggesting the team environment for them must be staged carefully. Also realize not all work needs to be done in groups; leaders should create an environment where individuality can be nourished as well as team work. Here's how to begin to accomplish "The development exchange: excessive team building for individual maverick appreciation."

STOP DOING THESE THINGS

1 Stop forcing all mavericks into primary team-player roles

Recognize the strength of mavericks lies in their quirky individuality, so pushing them full-force ahead into team-player positions may dampen too much of the characteristics you most want to nurture. In turn, the maverick's uncooperative tendencies may yield unproductive team dynamics which tend to worsen if the relationship is forced. Research findings indicate teammates perceive mavericks as independent souls who pursue their own agendas at the expense of the common good. The consequence is that mavericks may have conflict-ridden relationships with their teammates (Summers and Rosen, 1994). Our experiences dictate this most likely occurs when the team composition includes individuals who do not share the same core values about the work they do. If mavericks detect others don't understand the mission and don't feel the same intensity about achieving it as they do, trouble quickly brews. As mavericks sense others aren't even close to their intellectual capacity to solve the problem at hand, you may note their most difficult side pops out. Leaders, then, must stop putting mavericks into team roles that bring out the worst in their behavioral repertoire.

2 Stop creating conditions that stifle maverick creativity

By reducing flexibility in the organizational culture and requiring too much conformity, mavericks lose their zip. Most organizations have difficulty absorbing the maverick's creative problem-solving process into their culture. Creativity dies a slow, painful death in an overly structured environment full of rules and regulations, endless rounds of approval, strict dress codes, rigid office hours, highly prescribed assignments, and meaningless paperwork. Don't impose structure that isn't absolutely necessary.

> *Most organizations have difficulty absorbing the maverick's creative problem-solving process into their culture.*

Carefully watch the response to atypical, seemingly off-the-wall ideas you and others make. Observe existing team dynamics in your organization and watch for idea-smashing responses to "out-of-the-box" thinking. Are new ideas squashed before they can be explored? Peter Senge (1990) discovered in his research on the learning organization that most teams do not create new ideas. Rather, participants come with predetermined points of view and fight for those ideas to prevail. Decisions, then, are made by deference to the member who fights the hardest or makes the best argument. No new thought is generated. Box 7.2 shows phrases to stomp out of yours and others' response patterns.

▶▶ BOX 7.2 **Idea-smashing phrases**

"Let's send this to a committee for review."

"We've tried that and it didn't work before."

"We really already do something similar to what you're suggesting."

"That will never fly with upper management."

"It's a good idea, but . . ."

"This really isn't part of your job."

"Isn't this a bit extreme? Aren't you exaggerating?"

"You're way ahead of your time."

"No, that's the craziest thing I've ever heard!"

"This goes against our policies and procedures."

These phrases will put you on a dead-end course with mavericks by promoting what we call "organizational learned apathy."

---

3 Stop giving mavericks too much freedom

Sound like a contradiction: don't regulate, yet do restrict? The key word here is balance. Left with no guidelines, mavericks can run amok, causing more trouble than any leader can afford. While excessively holding back the reins can make matters worse, so can letting go too much. Other staff members may wonder why the maverick is given so much freedom while they are held to tighter boundaries. The perceived inequity may create undue motivational issues with other strong performers, so the leader of mavericks must be very careful not to be perceived as unfair by treating them too differently from other staff.

4 Stop neglecting to manage the maverick–organization interface

As the name implies, mavericks' ideas and behaviors may run counter a little, maybe a lot, to the culture of their organization. Mavericks, by definition, don't always play by the rules and may find themselves bumping into obstacles as they attempt to find their way through the maze of organizational rules, spoken and not. Don't count on them to figure out the system or maneuver it very well. If they were prone to conforming, they wouldn't be mavericks. Left to their own devices, they may end up derailed, rendered ineffective. Leaders must stop undermanaging the maverick–organization interface, thereby setting up disaster by not paving the way for the maverick's presentation of ideas. Too many mavericks have been lost in organizational space without the benefit of a support system.

5 Stop rewarding mavericks in conventional ways

Unconventional staff members may require unconventional reward and recognition methods. You won't usually find your mavericks lining up at the door to receive a brass and wood plaque during the annual company event. While they crave praise, just like most of us, the form of delivery must be well-orchestrated. Mavericks tend to steer clear of what they may consider to be the corny, even embarrassing, conventions of

> *To be effective with these free-spirited individuals you must break the mold and create more innovative reward strategies.*

organizational formalities. To be effective with these free-spirited individuals you must break the mold and create more innovative reward strategies.

6 Stop hiring to the status quo

Review the interview questions you typically ask and the answers that get your top candidates the most credit. Stop giving top marks to those who say all the right things by conventional standards. Stop looking for those who seem to fit the mold, sounding like they have been carefully schooled by a consultant in how to interview. Avoid dismissing those candidates who don't look like they've read the latest books on fashion in the workplace or surviving office politics.

Learning to lead rabble-rousing mavericks may be one of the greatest challenges you will face. We believe this ability is crucial to taking your organization out of the dark ages and into the exciting arena of creative, forward-thinking innovation. Here's what you can do now to nurture mavericks who may be stifled by the organizations in which they are struggling to survive.

START DOING THESE THINGS

1 Start choosing team assignments carefully and sparingly for mavericks

While we've established that mavericks are not the consummate team players a leader might yearn for, there is hope. When placed within the right composition of team members or in a carefully designed role, mavericks can show glimmers, even measurable quantities, of "teamability."

Mavericks will perform best when in a team with others they perceive as a creative and/or intellectual match. In other words, mavericks are a bit snobbish about who they want to ideate with around the team conference table. If the team assignment means deliberating with other mavericks, the tune they play may take on a different melody from what other team assignments produce. In a like-minded group, mavericks feel at home and more fully understood, freeing them to share their genius with other team members. A bond is established which allows atypical thinking to be the norm and, therefore, conformity is more tolerable to the maverick. Warren Bennis (Hesselbein and Cohen, 1999) found that the "great groups" he studied were made up of a unique construct of strong, often eccentric, individuals with a shared dream, so strong it causes them to abandon their egos in order to resolve conflict.

Another effective strategy for managing mavericks is to create specific and limited team roles designed to play to their strengths. Our experience teaches us that mavericks work well in teams when assigned "consultative" roles. These assignments require them to be on-call to their assigned teams, participating on an as-needed basis when their expertise is most crucial to the team's work. One insurance company we know created consultative roles for its three maverick-like actuaries who preferred to spend their days communing with their computers, crunching high-powered statistics. As part of a reorganization that created three customer-focused self-managing teams, one actuary was assigned to each team as a consulting member. When the team needed their expertise and creativity, they were called to meetings and expected to participate fully. Other team meetings were open to the actuaries if they chose to participate. The company found the mavericks were more likely to attend if they did not feel it was a requirement. And, when they were called to action, their interaction was highly productive.

2 Start developing an environment that stimulates creativity

First, you'll need to bolster your understanding of the creative process. Imagine you are facing an interesting situation: a donation of a 3000 square-foot home and 50 acres of land was given to the non-profit organization you lead. It is located about 70 miles south of the agency's main office. Jot down your ideas for what you might do with the property. Now, examine your list as a measure of your own creative problem-solving capability, utilizing the four creative abilities identified by Dr J. P. Torrance author of the Torrance Test of Creative Thinking:

- *Fluency*: How many ideas did you generate? Creative people typically produce more volume of ideas related to the problem than others might.
- *Flexibility*: How many categories of ideas were you able to bring forward? Rather than getting stuck on one type of idea, i.e. variations of a

conference/retreat center, creative minds can generate broader idea categories.

- *Originality:* How unusual were your ideas? Would most people, posed with the problem presented, think of the same ones? Generating unique thoughts is yet another signpost of creativity at work.

- *Elaboration:* How much detail did you write or envision as you ideated? The ability to expand an idea by adding detail is also characteristic of creativity.

Even if you have concluded creativity is not your personal strong suit, fine-tune your ability to identify, appreciate, and nurture those traits in others.

Next, understand what it takes for creativity to come forth. Jordan Ayan (1997), founder of Create-it! Inc., says four qualities are the heart of the creative spirit: curiosity, openness, risk tolerance, and energy. Applying these to organizational leadership requires creating an environment where these traits can flourish. Creative mavericks need permission to satisfy their curiosity by having time to "play" with problems and experimenting with ideas. 3M is famous for allowing its staff to utilize as much as 15 percent of their work time working on their own projects related to product development. Creative minds need to tinker. It is unlikely, then, you will foster creativity if you can't engineer some downtime for idea creation and incubation to occur. Faced with fierce time pressures, the creative process is stifled. Innovative ideas need time to grow. Protect the time of your creative mavericks.

Stimulate openness by providing continual sources of new ideas. Send your staff to conferences, seminars, and learning events of all varieties. Let them take field trips to other organizations to gain new perspectives. Bucking conventional organizational policies, which typically approve expenditures for job-related education, allows your staff to attend events outside their area of work. For example, let the marketing staff attend technical conferences; encourage the maintenance group to learn marketing skills; and, if you really want to go out on a limb, encourage them all to sign up for art classes. Don't let them get stuck in a job rut. Some leaders of creative types rotate their assignments among different product categories. By continually presenting new design challenges, creatives avoid losing their capacity for imagination (Caudron, 1994). Ensure the mavericks you lead are presented with a continual array of new, demanding, and interesting projects to keep that active mind engaged and working full steam ahead.

Allow for risk taking by being willing to say "yes" to implementation, at least via a pilot project, of ideas you don't fully understand or aren't sure you approve. We don't mean you should act foolishly. Establish boundaries around which risk taking can occur – i.e. adherence to policies, financial limitations of experimentation – then take a deep breath and turn your staff loose. Flipczak (1997) describes one company where staff members are encouraged to create new product lines by coming up with a business plan, demonstrating

> *Adopt a policy of saying, at least, "maybe" before you say "no" or let others squash new ideas.*

their financial competence. The plan must be approved before the new ideas are put in motion. Adopt a policy of saying, at least, "maybe" before you say "no" or let others squash new ideas. Try not to evaluate every new idea right out of the chute. Let the idea be cultivated a bit before you decide to cut it off.

Carefully monitor your response to a "failed" effort, once you've given the go-ahead for a risky idea to be born. Reframe the attempt as a learning experience and reward the effort. One plant manager we know does this with flair. When a group has taken a risk and flopped, he sends them a case of champagne with a laudatory note, saying , "Good try. Celebrate the learning." Distinguish between failure due to incompetence, which should be handled through performance feedback and joint problem solving, and failure due to a reasonable attempt to try something new. Some staff members can look like mavericks on the surface, but the competence and higher-order problem solving may be lacking.

Cultivate creative energy. What is it? The passion that drives the maverick – deeply held beliefs and standards that make work not only a way to earn a living, but a mission. Foster energy by talking about your own passion and listening intently to theirs. Inspire by keeping the mission and guiding principles of the organization in the forefront in all you do. Get excited with your mavericks, reinforcing those moments when creative energy is at its peak.

Consider broadening your focus. See if you can turn some of your borderline creative problem solvers into full-blown mavericks. Flipczak (1997) describes another company that has devised a kind of creativity center where staff can go to get their creative juices flowing. Comfy chairs, stars on the floor, and purple walls help to create an environment where staffs' creative ability can be stimulated. To provoke creative thoughts, staff are exposed to books, speakers, and videos designed to jolt them out of their "in-the-box" thinking patterns. Brainstorming sessions are offered, as well, to facilitate problem solving around challenging issues.

3 Start giving mavericks freedom with boundaries

Create the loosest boundaries your organizational culture will allow, then let the mavericks out of the corral. Mavericks typically wax and wane out of their productive periods, so they work best when work hours are minimally defined. "Anytime, anyplace" (*see* Chapter 8 on the "workplace exchange") is an optimal way of work for many mavericks, who may be unable to predict when their genius will get turned on. When giving assignments, be clear about the result expected, while avoiding dictating how the task must be done. If you're too specific, you might put your mavericks to sleep, taking away their freedom to exercise what they do best – solve problems creatively.

Mavericks may push the limits of convention. When they decide to surround themselves with rather unconventional decor or behavior, try not to gasp in horror. One maverick information systems group with whom we consulted had their cubicles packed full of sci-fi toys. Another maverick team we know begins each of its meetings with a unique ritual. They eat extremely smelly, pungent cheese contributed on a rotating basis by each team member. Another creative group collected tacky lamps from their travel: one with an Elvis shade, another full of glued-on sea shells, several lava lamps, and another full of peacock feathers. Go figure . . .

4 Start buffering your mavericks

The most important thing a leader of mavericks can do is to run interference for them, giving them some protection from the obstacles inherent in organizational life. Many leaders think they want creative, maverick types, but when such people arrive on the scene, the organizations really can't handle them proficiently. As a leader, you will need to provide a buffer if mavericks are to survive. If they slip up on the dress code one day, coming to work with an outfit just a little too funky for the suited administrative crowd they are scheduled to present to, quickly loan them a suit jacket and help them put together a presentable look! Don't make a big deal of it. If your mavericks have difficulty translating an idea into thought patterns interpretable by an operations group, intercede and help them make good sense. Or, should your maverick break an occasional rule and become noticed by upper management, smooth it over with the top brass and handle it privately. Assist your mavericks as they attempt to survive the often stifling effects of organizational politics.

More importantly, you may find that champion mavericks with forward-thinking ideas have trouble getting a voice within your organization. One of the curses of their having passion and vision is that they may be so far ahead of the pack, others can't relate to much of what they're saying. Mavericks with this profile often find others write them off as slightly loony and, therefore, discount them. Leaders must become advocates for their most passionate mavericks. Defend their right to explore cutting-edge, visionary ideas and give them the space to develop their thoughts. Assist them in putting their ideas into verbiage others can understand and appreciate.

5 | Start utilizing rewards that mavericks love

Constant reinforcement is essential in getting good work from all staff members, but especially from mavericks, who in spite of all the bravado, may be quite insecure. And, given they are typically ego-driven, make it clear to them you know they are special. Flattery will get you somewhere with the maverick.

The source of the recognition you give is critical. Mavericks most value praise that comes from someone they really respect, often people with a bit of "maverickism" in their blood, because then they know their work has been truly appreciated. How can a non-maverick evaluate the quality of their work? When a financial officer praises a designer, the credibility and its consequent impact is not nearly as great as when the art director praises a designer. Therefore, cue others to do some of the praising and recognizing you might typically do (unless, of course, you find yourself hosting maverick-like qualities).

For the most part, you can skip the formal reward program as a meaningful activity for most mavericks. They tend to view such events with disdain and suspicion, skipping out the back door just as soon as a lull in the program provides an opportunity. Many mavericks are a bit reticent when it comes to public display, so save the formal stuff for more conventional sorts.

Reward mavericks with adventuresome, unusual activities. Some toy manufacturers described by Caudron (1994) encourage their designers to get out and visit toy stores, trade shows, and playgrounds. They organize off-site meetings in imaginative places. Or they sit around plastic tables in their retail stores, brainstorming. One marketing group we worked with that designed food products for children, held its regular meetings at Camp Snoopy at the Mall of America in Minneapolis. By watching children and their parents interact in play, they began creating new product ideas more fluently than they had within the sterile walls of their corporate headquarters. Let your mavericks design some of their own professional development activities and don't be too quick to clamp down on unconventional ideas. Remember creativity requires stimulation from multiple sources, some far removed from the actual work the staff member may be doing.

Because their passion is their work, many mavericks host an enormous amount of intrinsic motivation. They are exhilarated by the opportunity to work in their fields. When placed in work environments known to be top in the field, the pride of being part of the best is reward enough in itself. Leaders can foster this type of work environment by building quality and performance, then making sure it is recognized professionally. Give mavericks the resources they need to present at professional conferences and publish their work, in order to build distinction for your work group. Be known as a great place to work because of state-of-the-art practices and innovations. Mavericks may flock to your door.

6 Start interviewing with the M-word in mind

If you're thinking by now that you've developed or inherited a rather traditional, status quo group of staff, consider recruiting more maverick-like talent. This will require developing an interview approach that probes carefully with the questions we suggest to see if you've found a live one! Listen for answers that are not typical and that show imagination. Throw out the usual interview criterion of "organizational fit" and entertain embracing "organizational misfit" if you want to bring in some new blood. We don't mean, however, that you should look for extreme non-conformists. Simply challenge your run-of-the-mill assumptions about what makes a good staff member and beef-up your capacity to tolerate more diversity of style and thought. Box 7.3 provides maverick-detecting interview questions.

> **Listen for answers that are not typical and that show imagination.**

> **BOX 7.3** **Maverick-detecting interview questions**

Q: *How do you typically go about solving a problem?*

Maverick-like answer: I spend a great deal of time detecting the cause of the problem, working intensely, sometimes oblivious to others around me. Once I've discovered the cause, I begin to toy with optional solutions, testing each one until I find the answer. Sometimes I mull the problem over for several days before the answer comes to me.

Q: *What drives you to work in this field?*

Maverick-like answer: I have an intense passion for my work. It's really not work, it's my life's purpose. Some people think I'm a workaholic. I see myself as on a mission.

Q: *What is your vision of the future for your field of work?*

Maverick-like answer: (for a training position) It is clear to me we won't even recognize training programs as we know them today ten years from now. Learning will be delivered to staff members' fingertips via virtual 3D space in on-line learning environments so exciting and interactive, we will never again think education is dull!

Q: *How have you developed your creative problem-solving abilities?*

Maverick-like answer: I have a broad range of interests. Many are outside my field of study. I am curious about everything and like to explore new endeavors. I like challenges and seek them out in my hobbies as well as my work.

Q: *How do you get others to understand the ideas you develop?*

Maverick-like answer: Most organizations I have worked in have put up a lot of barriers for me. Frankly, I'm sometimes thought of as outrageous because I think outside of the status quo and have a lot of passion for what I belief in. I relate best to those in my own field who have the same mission and vision as I do. Others have a hard time understanding me, at times. I am not very tolerant of organizational politics. My focus is on my work. I do best when someone else runs interference for me.

While teams are important organizational units, our point is simply this: don't overdo a good thing. Trying to stuff mavericks into team boxes that just aren't the right size may stunt creativity you and your organization desperately need to lead the next innovation in product or service. Expand your options as you think about how best to use the talent each individual staff member holds and develop your tolerance for a little quirkiness. Use both teams *and* individual assignments to accomplish the goals. And, when you feel it necessary to include mavericks in teams, stage the group carefully, utilizing the guidelines we've provided in this chapter. Box 7.4 gives a summary of "The development exchange: excessive team building for individual maverick appreciation."

>> BOX 7.4   **The development exchange: excessive team building for individual maverick appreciation**

Stop	Start
1 Forcing all mavericks into primary team-player roles.	1 Choosing team assignments carefully and sparingly for mavericks.
2 Creating conditions that stifle maverick creativity.	2 Developing an environment that stimulates creativity.
3 Giving mavericks too much freedom.	3 Giving them freedom with boundaries.
4 Neglecting to manage the maverick–organizational interface.	4 Buffering your mavericks.
5 Rewarding mavericks in conventional ways.	5 Utilizing rewards that mavericks love.
6 Hiring to the status quo.	6 Interviewing with the M-word in mind.

To help you gain further insight on leading mavericks and appreciating the important role they have to play in organizations, meet Michael Osterholm.

A maverick leader

Michael Osterholm, Ph.D., MPH,
Chairman and CEO, Infection Control Advisory Network, Inc.
(former Minnesota State Epidemiologist, and Chief, Acute Disease and Epidemiology Section, Minnesota Department of Health)

One of the leading epidemiologists in the United States, Michael Osterholm is known as a superb scientist, detecting and preventing infectious diseases with an uncanny sleuth-like ability. He is an outspoken public health activist, passionate in his view that emerging infectious diseases pose a serious threat to world safety. Sometimes pegged a doomsayer, Dr Osterholm is passionate in his belief that bioterrorism constitutes a real and grave danger world-wide, yet is not being given serious attention by government officials.

Q *How would you define the term "maverick"?*

A It's a hard term to understand. Some think mavericks just go against the grain. For me, I go with the *data*, letting it guide me to the conclusions I draw and represent in my viewpoints. Mavericks are probably born with more of a sense of vision than others.

Q *What do you mean by more of a sense of vision?*

A Like a good baseball or football player, the ability to predict the future or have vision is often innate. For example, I recognized the changing threat of food-borne diseases, AIDS, infectious disease issues in daycare, and, now, bioterrorism years before they became real. The vision is both a blessing and a curse. Saying or talking about things that seem revolutionary when they are not an issue at the time is often hard for others to relate to. Mavericks have a sixth sense. They take three or four pieces of data and integrate them to see a bigger picture, anticipate the future, and then make decisions.

Q *How can leaders develop more of this ability in their staff?*

A First, recruit people who will challenge you. Look for candidates who have vision. Ask them, "What is your vision?" Then, foster mavericks by giving them some latitude. I have had managers who have buffered me by taking the heat for tough, sometimes politically unpopular decisions I have made or actions I have taken.

Q *How do you develop maverick-like behavior in your staff?*

A I duplicate how I have been treated. I don't have a plan for people. I don't try to direct the wind; I adjust to each individual's needs at any given time. I surround myself with people who have the same ideals and reward them for pursuing those ideals.

Q *How can organizations create a climate for mavericks to thrive?*

A They should value real leadership but understand it will result in discomfort, criticism, and confusion. Expect that and it won't be troublesome when it happens. The best supervisors of mavericks are probably not mavericks themselves, but those who know how to manage them. You can't have all mavericks in a work unit. I think good managers of mavericks live vicariously through them; they enjoy and value the maverick's crusade. It's a partnership. More specifically, leaders of mavericks can provide an anchor by encouraging and supporting them. Leaders should hold them to a standard – mavericks, to be effective, have to be more than a puff of smoke; they have to show results.

Q *Can mavericks work successfully in teams?*

A Absolutely. If all team members have mutual understanding and deep-felt respect for what they are doing, a maverick will work well in the team. The key is that all the team members have to have the same vision and complementary skills. Mavericks don't "suffer fools" well and, therefore, don't work as effectively with those that don't share their passion. Mavericks don't do well with whininess, either. If there is something wrong, they move on and fix it. Maverick success most often comes from teamwork, partnerships with those above and below you in the organization. If I didn't have people to help me execute my ideas, I would be lost.

REFERENCES

Ayan, J. (1997) *Aha! 10 Ways to Free Your Creative Sprit and Find Your Great Ideas*. New York: Crown Trade Paperbacks.

Caudron, S. (1994) "Strategies for managing creative workers," *Personnel Journal*, 73 (12), 104–13.

Flipczak, B. (1997) "It takes all kinds: Creativity in the work force," *Training*, 34 (5), 32–40.

Hesselbein, F. and Cohen, P. (Eds) (1999) *Leader to Leader: Enduring insights from the Drucker Foundation's award winning journal*. San Francisco: Jossey-Bass.

Senge, P. (1990) *The Fifth Discipline*. New York: Doubleday.

Summers, L. and Rosen, B. (1994) "Mavericks ride again," *Training and Development*, 48 (5), 119–124.

Torrance, E. P. (1966) *Torrance Tests of Creative Thinking*. Bensenville, IL: Scholastic Testing Service.

8

THE WORKPLACE EXCHANGE

Stationary edifices for mobile and virtual environments

C onstance Lockhart, Division Director for Internal and External Communications in a governmental agency, is at her desk examining the blueprints for the office space her 80-member staff now occupies. With an anticipated 20 percent increase in staff coming on board in the next three months, Constance must find room for them in the already crowded quarters the Division utilizes. Currently, the office configuration includes a multiple-cubicle bank in the center of the floor space, surrounded by larger private offices with windows. Two of the perimeter offices serve as conference rooms, often in demand since the Division utilizes a project-team structure. Constance scans the blueprints looking for places to add more cubicles, then searches the drawings of the entire building trying to find more available square footage. She realizes she will have to move nearly every staff member in order to get team members in reasonable proximity to one another. She notes she must also add more meeting and classroom space, since learning is becoming a critical element in keeping her staff abreast of new developments. As Constance begins plotting the remodeling that will be necessary, she becomes keenly aware of the time consumption and financial commitment this space change will devour. And she realizes the resistance she'll face as staff are moved to new work areas, since many are comfortable in the offices they now inhabit.

Constance is going down a common path to staff growth and workplace reconfiguration. She is thinking traditionally, assuming she must add more cubicles, meeting rooms, and square footage to handle her office needs. There's a whole new world of options for Constance, which can help her prepare her organization to add and subtract staff many times with minimal disruption. Before calling the construction crew, Constance should begin now to explore mobile, virtual workplace development, reducing her focus on stationary, non-flexible configurations. Here's what she should consider.

LIMITATIONS OF STATIONARY, NON-FLEXIBLE WORK ENVIRONMENTS

As our interviewees taught us, effective leaders today must develop a flexible workforce linked by technology and organized to maximize productivity through effective communication and teamwork. Traditional office space, equipment, and configuration inhibit a leader's ability to accomplish those goals.

Most office space isn't conducive to group work and team communication. It segregates people into private spaces, removes departments and divisions from one another, and puts team members in inconvenient locations to one another. As teams are disbanded and new ones formed, traditional office space is typically not designed to "migrate" with these transitions. Divisions and departments are evolving, more and more, into project teams and *ad hoc* task forces. The walls are tumbling down figuratively, but they need to come down literally!

Additionally, many offices have not been "wired" to meet the needs of rapidly expanding virtual work. Without an appropriate technological infrastructure, virtual staff members cannot work effectively, and their efficiency and productivity are reduced when they have to work across geographic boundaries with archaic mechanisms. We have been impressed to discover so many teams within our client populations working productively with minimal technology, but we also recognize the limitations leaders put in front of these groups when a bit more sophistication could mean enormous gains in work efficiency and output.

It's time for leaders to stop perpetuating work environments that are more appropriate for the chain-of-command age than today's fluid, flatter, on-line work environments. Leaders must stop doing these things now. "The workplace exchange: stationary edifices for mobile and virtual environments" will show you the way.

STOP DOING THESE THINGS

1 Stop constructing office buildings as the only means of space expansion

Resist the urge to call a construction crew every time you need more space. Buildings simply generate more overhead and may not be the most forward-thinking solution to space expansion. In fact, office buildings as we know them today are becoming more and more obsolete. A growing percentage of work is being done in places other than traditional offices – homes, automobiles, lobbies, airline clubs, customer sites and virtually, on-line.

William Stott, Facilities and Services Director at Andersen Consulting's Paris office, told us:

> *Many of our consultants spend 80 percent of their time outside the office. Is there any reason to justify they occupy one private space 100 percent of the time? Our environment is one where the consultants can find the type of space and services they need for the time they need it. We have moved from providing each person with 10 to 15 square meters to shared space of over 7000 square meters. In this kind of environment, consultants have the possibility of using any type of space best suited to their needs (such as open workspaces, informal meeting rooms, private interview spaces, comfortable lounges, and client meeting rooms).*
>
> *This initiative not only provides a better quality environment for our staff and clients, it allows us to nearly double our head count, yet keep the same amount of space. We found it saved us approximately $1 million per year by using space in more efficient ways.*

So, stop assuming all work must be done in an office building and begin to think of alternative spaces for getting tasks done. In fact, stop using the term office and replace it instead with workspace, a more appropriate term to describe the many alternatives available.

2 Stop being chintzy

As staff members work in atypical locations, technological equipment becomes their lifeline to the organization. Virtual workplace efforts can be marginalized if organizations are unwilling to invest in the technology to make a home office purr. Give your staff members more than a telephone line and a fax. Many companies will not cover the cost of computers and fax machines. Nor do they provide technical assistance when the telecommuter's system goes down in the middle of a critical 57–page report (Warner, 1997). Don't make it so hard on those pioneering new ways of work.

3 Stop putting up walls

Some of you may be cringing about now as you recall the era of open office plans, which ran rampant in the United States in the last 25 years. Silicon Valley began erecting office buildings, but no walls, forcing staff members to do their work in an entirely open space, filled with rows of desks. The noise and commotion caused many organizations to abandon the open plan and put the walls back up just about as quickly as they had been dismantled.

But it's a whole new world in workspace design. Today's furniture manufacturers offer some creative alternatives that will truly let the walls come tumbling down. We'll introduce you to them later in this chapter.

4 Stop living in dullsville

Discard the old notion that workplaces have to be designed strictly for putting your nose to the grindstone. Sterile cubicles, white walls with wildlife art and tan carpeting aren't the sole elements of appropriate office decor. Stop thinking about office interiors in a totally functional manner. Boring space doesn't do much to enhance staff members' motivation and spirit.

> *Stop thinking about office interiors in a totally functional manner.*

5 Stop segregating learning from day-to-day work

In traditional workplaces, learning takes place in classrooms on- and off-site. The learning environment tends to be contained in separate spaces, removed from the staff person's work station. While some of this educational delivery mode may still have merit, stop using it exclusively. It may not provide immediate enough learning opportunities to meet the ongoing, day-to-day needs of a workforce that must stay current as information availability frequently explodes.

6 Stop minimizing ergonomics

As workspace becomes more sophisticated, leaders must stop assuming any chair, computer station, and table will do. They must check any tendency to show minimal concern for air flow, noise pollution, and lighting. Neglect of working conditions can make you the target of more worker compensation claims and even lawsuits than you have time and money to deal with.

7 Stop assuming you must see staff to manage them

One of the commonly held beliefs we hear espoused by leaders attending our seminars is, "We can't manage staff unless we can see their eyeballs." In other words, many leaders don't really think it is possible to manage someone fully whom they can't see each day. Our interviews and experiences tell us that many leaders have mastered this capability; it is possible to lead remote staff and do it admirably. Sometimes the resistance is due to lack of trust of what staff will do if the leader isn't looming around in the same building. Sometimes it is the leaders' concern that they will forget about staff they don't bump into in the hallways. We wonder, though, how often leaders really see their staff if they are housed in the same facility! So, cast off any negative assumptions you may have about the feasibility of remote leadership.

8 Stop living by old workplace rules

Many management courses have taught the following rules of organizational politics and power:

- having more space and windows means you have more power;
- dressing in the "corporate uniform" suggests you have more status and/or gives you more credibility;
- using commanding gestures to dominate at the conference table indicates power;
- schmoozing around the water fountain is an important way to get in on the informal communication network and really know what's going on;
- being seen in the right places raises your visibility and enhances your organizational influence.

143

With the advent of more on-line work where how someone looks and behaves may not even be known, these rules come into question. Begin, now, to discard any conventional notions about power and politics and learn the new rules of virtual organizational life.

START DOING THESE THINGS

1 Start creating virtual office and telecommuting capability

Telecommuting (in Europe, it's called "teleworking") changes the way people work by breaking down the notion that everyone must come to a workplace at about the same time every day. Rather than moving people to the work, the work is moved, primarily through technology, to the people who will do it, thus creating the virtual office. At one company described in a *Business Week* article (Baig, 1995), all 240 core sales staff members are telecommuters outfitted with groupware (networking and meeting software), digital telephone lines and wide-ranging cellular networks. They are directed to work anytime, anyplace, as long as it is *not* in the office. New York-based Link Resources, which tracks telecommuting and virtual office trends, predicts that the number of Americans telecommuting will swell from 7.6 million in 1994 to 25 million in the year 2000 (Greengard, 1994). Nearly all the leaders we interviewed reported rapidly increasing numbers of both internal and external staff who telecommute.

The advantages of telecommuting are numerous. Studies proclaim telecommuters outperform their peers in a traditional office by approximately 16 percent, spending much less time in unproductive meetings. They report fewer interruptions and most just plain like it. The Institute for the Study of Distributed Work estimates a savings of two dollars for every one dollar invested by an organization in remote equipment and extra telephone lines required to get a telecommuter started. The 1990 revisions of the Clean Air Act requires employers with more than 100 staff members at a given site to reduce employee trips to work if the business is located in a polluted city. Telecommuting not only reduces pollution, it potentially eliminates the morning and late afternoon traffic jam. Telecommuting

> *Telecommuting allows an organization to recruit the best staff members from anywhere in the world.*

allows an organization to recruit the best staff members from anywhere in the world. And, telecommuting means not having to move staff, saving relocation costs (Hequet, 1994).

One consultant we know who works on contract for a number of client organizations delights in her home office, savoring the one to two days she spends there each week. While she finds she must utilize childcare resources to allow her to focus fully on her work, she can simultaneously work at her computer, do the laundry, and give her pets the attention they deserve! Better yet, she can do all of this while comfortable in her sweatsuit, the ulti- mate in casual day! Many telecommuters work outside the parameters of usual work hours, interchanging work with play and chores. Some have reported to us they work into the wee hours of the morning or begin before the sun rises. They work when they are most productive.

Telecommuting is not without its potential problems. Some staff mem- bers may abuse the freedom or manage it poorly, allowing too many interruptions at the telecommuting site. For some, isolation from face-to- face contact may make telecommuting from home undesirable. Jack Johnson, Chief Operating Officer of Teltech, a research and knowledge man- agement services company in Minneapolis, employs numerous staff who work off-site. He told us the best remote staff persons are those who are self- confident, not highly extroverted, and self-initiating. They are patient, not jumping to conclusions when they don't get complete information. Teltech keeps its remote staff linked with the company by including them in peri- odic team-training sessions, by having special meetings solely for remote staff members, and by e-mailing company information weekly and announcing good news via universal voice mail. When Teltech executives travel, they visit remote staff. Through audioconferences as well as periodic visits to corporate headquarters, off-site staff participate in team meetings.

Many telecommuters will work from a home office while others will station themselves at "hotels", temporary offices complete with concierge services. Hotellers can call ahead to these sites to schedule an office for a given period of time and arrive to find their name on an office door and the equipment requested set up, ready to go. Many hotel sites provide dry cleaners, shoe repair, take-out food and, of course, a fitness center. Some organizations will create their own hotels in the form of satellite offices while others will share hotel space. Still others may reserve some spare offices in their own main office location for telecommuters. This type of space, often called "free addresses", will be used on a first-come, first-served basis. Chris Rence, Information Technology Director, Global Solution Office of Andersen Consulting's Minneapolis office, spoke of the cost effectiveness and efficiencies of having a group of offices that can be reserved by staff not on-site full time: "It's very effective space management because we don't have enough space for every person. By rotating this space when they're not there, it saves you costs by not having 'dark offices' because someone's out of town."

Greengard (1994) describes a 30,000-square-foot converted warehouse near downtown Los Angeles equipped with state-of-the art offices, conference rooms, free parking, and convenient freeway access. Several companies lease space there for telecommuters and others to work in their own community and avoid long commutes. Other companies located in large cities across the United States have set up satellite offices on the outskirts to reduce their staff members' commute time and provide more convenience.

Hotel sites might also include the customer's office. One company dramatically reduced the time it takes to work up a draft of a proposed office design by having salespeople work right in the customer's office, a model many organizations are utilizing with their vendors and suppliers as well (Martin, 1996).

2 Start installing appropriate virtual office tools

The basic virtual office tools are simple: a computer and telephone. The computer in most cases must include an intranet, a secure information-sharing system for accessing internal organizational data. Many display commonly used information, incorporate groupware for team data-sharing and problem solving, and track sales and customer requests.

Desktop conferencing software will soon include video PC capabilities, which allow visual images to accompany both written and voice communication. When this technology becomes more typical, we predict telecommuters will experience much less isolation and feel more able to develop personal relationships through on-line communication. And managers will no longer be able to claim they can't supervise telecommuters because they can't see them! Chapter 6 gives a further description of these systems and their application to virtual team building.

While waiting for desktop conferencing to be incorporated into personal computers, make sure your organization has access to videoconferencing facilities and utilizes them regularly. While we find many of our client

organizations have videoconferencing capability, it is often underutilized.
Refer to Chapter 3 on the "communication exchange" for videoconferencing
guidelines.

3 Start adapting your main office site

We don't expect all work will be done from remote workspaces. Most of the
human resource directors we interviewed concur that in the next few years
organizations are more likely to use a combination of off-site and on-site
staff members. But the main workspace, to accommodate new forms of
work, will look different from the way it does today. While job descriptions
become a thing of the past, and flexible assignments become more of the
norm, workspace will need to reflect these changes. Start re-inventing your
home office workspace, considering the following options, which we discovered in our tour of Dayton's Commercial Interiors in Minneapolis.

Caves and commons

Steelcase and other furniture manufacturers have developed total work environments, fitted with hook-ups for all needed technology, designed to move

Fig 8.1 ■ Caves and commons
Source: Courtesy of Steelcase Inc., Grand Rapids, Michigan, USA

with the worker. Just like in the Wild West, staff members can then "pull up their wagons" around commons, a central team space. These units can be reconfigured time and time again as new teams form and others adjourn. Yet staff members do not have to "move" their belongings to new physical space.

Communications centers

To service the "cave dwellers", many organizations will use communications centers complete with television, fax, newspapers, and tables for impromptu meetings. Another variation is the "huddle room" for team brainstorming sessions, sometimes equipped, as one hospital administrator we know did, with toys, problem-solving puzzles, creativity games, and comic video tapes to spur on teams to greater innovation and fun!

Team suites

Complete with a project or group address, team suites typically include private office space, some assigned, some unassigned. These include meeting areas complete with electronic whiteboards, storage space, and, in some cases, espresso bars.

Fig 8.2 ■ Team suite
Source: Courtesy of Steelcase Inc., Grand Rapids, Michigan, USA

Escalators

To promote conversation, escalators may be more desirable than traditional elevators. One company outside Cincinnati has a new office building that hosts escalators to transport staff between floors because elevators are viewed as too "chat-zapping" (Hamilton with Baker and Vlasic, 1996).

Everything on wheels

"Free address lockers" resemble armoires on wheels with computer, files, telephone, desktop, and docking unit which houses required electronics. These units can be wheeled into empty office spaces for short-term or long-term usage.

Forum spaces

Sitting areas, usually created in open spaces like hallways, lobbies, alcoves, and outdoors, are designed to encourage spontaneous discussions or provide a space for informal meetings. According to Mark Eklund, President of Dayton's Commercial Interiors, "These gathering spaces are starting to look more like residential kitchens and up-scale coffee houses. These will attract generation Xers who aren't into status as much as performance opportunities, coolness, and learning – all in one 'learn-and-talk' environment."

As you make choices about which of these options to embrace, ask yourself the following questions:

- How much private space and interactive space does each staff person and group need?
- How can I maximize space utilization to accommodate the growing trend for more staff members to be doing at least part of their work off-site?
- How can I create the most flexible physical work environment to avoid getting caught with space mismatched to workforce needs?
- Does the workspace configuration match the type of work (i.e. team-based) the staff is actually performing?

4 Start adding some pizzazz

As we visited a variety of non-traditional workplaces, we discovered many additional elements that add sparkle, fun, and play to the work environment.

Some firms are creating running or walking tracks around banks of work stations so people can get exercise and, at the same time, move from one department to another without feeling like they are crossing a demilitarized zone (Lieber, 1996). Others are installing full-fledged health clubs for workouts, massage, as well as personal training and nutritional counseling.

Other interesting additions to the workspace include pool tables for stress reduction, franchised coffee shops on site, cybercafés complete with computers and CNN, and knowledge centers for accessing information with the assistance of a cybrarian, an updated version of a librarian. The possibilities are endless.

5 Start integrating on-call learning capability

As you develop a more geographically dispersed workforce, traditional classroom training methods will become more cumbersome and costly. The

> *Training must fit the fast-paced, flexible workforce of the 21st century, providing information at the moment it is needed.*

World Wide Web, intranet systems, and interactive TV offer high-tech distance learning solutions to ensure the workforce can readily access training opportunities. Training must fit the fast-paced, flexible workforce of the 21st century, providing information at the moment it is needed.

Distance learning includes two main categories. First, synchronous instruction involves the simultaneous participation of learners and teachers in real time with face-to-face (via video) or voice-to-voice interaction. Second, asynchronous learning is a mode that allows learners to access instruction individually at their own convenience. They need only have access to the Internet or intranet and an e-mail account (*Distance Learning*, 1996).

At a West Coast company that supplies parts for chipmaking and other equipment, a supervisor's time spent on training new staff has been dramatically decreased by the use of the newest training aid. An interactive computer program spells out, step-by-step with color graphics, how to assemble its machines. This "electronic mentor" works side-by-side to review immediately instructions at the learner's request. At other companies, as well, the traditional classroom complete with its lectures and live instructors has been ditched and replaced with 3-D virtual-reality simulators in which machinery simply stops working if the trainee makes a critical mistake, ensuring highly relevant, individualized learning (Bylinsky, 1996).

Intranet and Internet technology allows education and training to be delivered directly to staff members' desktops as long as they have access to a computer. By logging on at a given time, they can partake of college and university courses from many institutions around the world. Or, by installing courses developed internally or purchased from the outside into the corporate intranet, staff can learn at their own convenience. Yet another model might be simply to turn on the television and watch training delivered via satellite networks, either live or via video. Mike Peterson, Senior Vice-President of Merchandise Planning and Merchandise Presentation at the Department Store Division of Dayton-Hudson Corporation, reports:

> *We do CD-ROM training in the stores and it's worked very well for us there. Over 200,000 team members have been trained using this type of technology. They can test their knowledge and the effectiveness of the training immediately and individually. We're also using the intranet for complete documentation and support for our new merchandising systems. People with questions can find information at their fingertips, all hyper-linked and searchable without having to pore over old-fashioned manuals.*

The advantages of the ever more virtualized classroom are numerous. Anytime, anyplace training accommodates variable work hours, lifestyles, and telecommuting practices. It allows staff members to control their own learning by pacing instruction to meet their individual needs. And, in most cases, it is cost effective. Depending on the degree of sophistication, an hour's worth of instruction can cost $15,000 to $200,000 for a design company to prepare. However, authoring software programs allow staff members inside an organization to prepare their own computer-based training at costs estimated at the low end of this range (Bylinsky, 1996).

Begin now to create systems for delivering education and training directly to yourself and your staff. Reduce your usage of the traditional classroom mode and invent ways to put electronic coaches at everyone's side. Estimates are that multimedia training will more than double by 2000 and that one in two staff members will have multimedia workstations

(Salopek, 1998). Infuse your organizational environment with independent and team-learning devices: data bases, CD-ROMs, videos, and access to on-line courseware and interaction. Make learning an everyday occurrence.

6 Start thinking ergonomically

As you redesign and reconfigure your organization's workspace, don't forget to think carefully about the safety and comfort of your staff, both on-site and off-site. Studies have shown that productivity is increased at the same time costly workers' compensation claims are decreased, when ergonomically correct workstations are customized to the needs of each staff person.

The ergonomically correct and cost-effective work station includes the following (Bencivenga, 1996):

- location near a window
- bright carpets held down by glue with little odor
- flexible, ergonomic chairs that can be adjusted for seat and arm height and back tension
- work stations that can be altered for height and with adjustable keyboard trays
- glare screens for computer monitors
- task lights for reading printed material
- dimmer system that adjusts indoor light to compensate for sunlight within the room
- clean, well-maintained ventilation system that provides high levels of oxygen within the building.

Consider an innovative approach like the Discovery Room at Mayo Clinic in Rochester, Minnesota. There, staff can come to "play" with a variety of personal office environments to find options best suited for them. The room's specially developed desk allows staff to experience the effects of different positions, adjust the chair in a variety of angles, and tilt the keyboard until the optimum combination is found (Kirchner, 1997).

7 Start learning to manage staff you don't see

Our interviews and experiences have taught us it is not imperative that managers co-locate with the staff they manage. Leading telecommuters and virtual staff members requires many of the same skill sets used face-to-face, plus some additional critical competencies.

Choose the right people for the right reasons. In our seminars we often hear people say they would like to telecommute for all the wrong reasons: to cut down on daycare expenses by keeping the pre-schoolers at home, to sleep-in a couple days a week, to be there when the children get home from school, or to catch up on Oprah. The answer you want to hear from your staff members is this: "I want to work at home to have less distractions and be more productive." While flexibility is a benefit of telecommuting, it should not be the driving cause. Recognize that working at home is not for everyone. The best telecommuters are self-starters who can motivate themselves well enough to stay away from the many distractions of the home environment. And, they are savvy enough to develop a network of relationships in the main office, so being out of site is not a handicap.

Make sure off-site staff are well-trained. Training should include the set-up and use of equipment, safety and ergonomics, and time management. Telecommuters may need to be reminded that the anytime, anyplace work style can turn into every time, every place. Some organizations offer specific classes on how to work virtually, including how to stay motivated at home, self-management skills, and avoiding procrastination. Similarly, courses are offered for managers in how to lead in a virtual environment, including topics like establishing performance contracts, monitoring off-site staff, and keeping telecommuters in touch with the organization (Slobodzian, 1996). Box 8.1 provides additional guidelines for telecommuters.

Delineate a performance contract. Detail the tasks to be accomplished, performance standards, and timelines. Include a schedule for on-line meetings and expectations for coming into the main office. Most studies indicate local telecommuters should come in, on the average, once per week. As telecommuting becomes more standard, we predict face-to-face interactions will occur even less frequently.

Within the boundaries established, let telecommuters work when they want. Discard your conventional notions that work must be done on a schedule; free telecommuters to work on tasks when they choose. Some

> **►► BOX 8.1** **Guidelines for telecommuters**

- Make sure you have some visibility in your organization, especially if you are a new hire. Attend events, show up at meetings. If you are local, work in the main office once each week at least part of a day.
- Take home twice as much work as you typically get done in a day at the main office.
- If telecommuting from home, set up a separate office space and arrange daycare. Don't assume you can take care of the household and children while working.
- Develop a signed agreement with your employer that covers safety, work hours, insurance, and job expectations.
- Make sure job expectations are clear. Know what you are expected to do and on what time frame. Then deliver, flawlessly.
- Check in by telephone, fax or e-mail frequently, letting others know what you're working on. Maintain a presence, from a distance.
- Schmooze on-line and via telephone. Don't neglect the need to develop relationships.

may prefer working in the middle of the night while others may like the rigor of a more traditional daily routine. As long as the job expectations are being met, stay out of the way.

Don't forget to recognize and reward. Use on-line communication for more than just passing work back and forth. Just as you would with staff you see more frequently, send messages of praise, a bit of humor now and again, an encouraging word or two. Think of yourself as an on-line coach. One virtual team member we know rarely sees her supervisor or spends time in the main office. Yet she receives a daily cheerleading message on her laptop so she always feels her team leader is nearby, encouraging her efforts. Additional "how tos" for leading telecommuters are presented in Box 8.2.

8 Start recognizing the new workplace will mean new organizational rules

In the virtualized work world, the new workplace will change the way

Workspace will become a social tool, focusing on activities, not titles.

we think about organizational politics. Power will be defined less by the space you inhabit or the "dress for success" style and demeanor you've acquired and more by the work you produce and

---

> **BOX 8.2** **Guidelines for leading telecommuters**

- Make sure to bring telecommuters to the main office periodically. If they are local, consider a weekly visit the norm.
- Consider assignments amenable to telecommuting – essentially any job that does not require staff to be in the office daily.
- Start your telecommuting initiative with a pilot program; provide participants with an option to return to the main office if it doesn't work out to their satisfaction or to yours.
- Communicate frequently. Keep telecommuters up to date on the latest developments in the organization.
- Include telecommuters in training and development activities. Treat them like any other staff member.
- Make sure leaders visit remote sites and telecommuters periodically.
- Make sure telecommuters hear good news via e-mail and voice mail.

---

the knowledge for which you're known. The old rules dictated that the more physical space, square footage, and windows staff obtained, then the greater status and power base they had in the organization. These rules will no longer be in operation as space becomes virtualized. Leaders, then, are more likely to be in the middle of the action, coordinating on-line networks of information flow, rather than isolated from the hub of activity. Workspace will become a social tool, focusing on activities, not titles.

Leaders functioning within more virtualized work environments will find they may not afford the accouterments of well-appointed office space. Their power base will come from the results for which they are known and the skills and wisdom they have attained, as well as the ability to lead astutely a workforce often separated by physical space and connected by technology. Professional image will come from the virtual presence the leader creates through masterful use of a combination of on-line communication abilities and high-impact face-to-face interactions.

Build a workplace using "The workplace exchange: stationary edifices for mobile and virtual environments," summarized in Box 8.3. To see how one organization utilizes the workplace exchange, review the profile of Andersen Consulting's Paris office, and its flexible approach to workspace.

>> BOX 8.3 **The workplace exchange:
stationary edifices for mobile and virtual environments**

Stop	*Start*
1 Constructing office buildings as the only means of space expansion.	**1** Creating virtual office and telecommuting capability.
2 Being chintzy.	**2** Installing appropriate virtual office tools.
3 Putting up walls.	**3** Adapting your main office site.
4 Living in dullsville.	**4** Adding some pizzazz.
5 Segregating learning from day-to-day work.	**5** Integrating on-call learning capability.
6 Minimizing ergonomics.	**6** Thinking ergonomically.
7 Assuming you must see staff to manage them.	**7** Learning to manage staff you don't see.
8 Living by old workplace rules.	**8** Recognizing the new workplace will mean new organizational rules.

ORGANIZATIONAL PROFILE

A flexible workspace
Andersen Consulting's Paris office

The Andersen Consulting Paris office, which opened in January 1998 at 55 avenue George V, was the pioneering office for the flexible workspace concept. This office enabled Andersen Consulting Paris to grow from 1200 in 1996 to 2000 people in 1998. The latest technology and processes have been combined with a common communications network throughout all the offices worldwide.

The top floor is dedicated to client meetings and all the meeting rooms can be provided with the necessary technological equipment, food, and beverage. The fourth floor houses internal meeting rooms, including an auditorium with a capacity for 100 people.

There are four floors dedicated to the Practice, where consultants occupy 200 open workspaces on a reservation basis. Each consultant has a rolling cabinet which is delivered to their reserved workspace during the night. All Practice floors are fully equipped with faxes, photocopiers, stationery and refreshments, as well as data and voice cabling, facilitating communication with other offices and clients.

The first floor is called the "Lounge" and contains a Club Space which was conceived after the idea of a first class airport lounge. This floor contains a variety of short-term, non-reservable spaces such as touch-down spaces, smoking and non-smoking lounges, and services such as you would find in a five-star hotel (Guest Relations, Reservations, Concierge).

All personnel who enter the building check in at an interactive kiosk with their card. This enables them to check their reservations for the day and to obtain other information on who is in the building and which meetings are taking place that day. They check out in the same way every time they leave the building, enabling the Communication Center to know whether they are present or not.

Everyone working in the building displays self-regulation and, most importantly, self-accountability for space and services used. In addition, the common look and feel throughout the building create a strong visual symbol of Andersen Consulting's culture and identity.

REFERENCES

Baig, E. (1995) "Welcome to the officeless office," *Business Week*, 26 June, 104–5.

Bencivenga, D. (1996) "The economics of ergonomics," *HRMagazine*, 41 (8), 68–75.

Bylinsky, G. (1996) "Training staff better, faster, and cheaper," *Fortune*, 134 (5), 172A–I.

"Distance learning", *Fast Forward*, 1996, December, 1.

Greengard, S. (1994) "Making the virtual office a reality," *Personnel Journal*, 73 (9), 67–79.

Hamilton, J. with Baker, S. and Vlasic, B. (1996) "The new workplace," *Business Week*, Issue 3473, 107–17.

Hequet, M. (1994) "How telecommuting transforms work," *Training*, 31 (11), 57–61.

Kirchner, D. (1997) "The shape of things to come," *WorldTraveler*, May, 55–7, 76.

Lieber, R. (1996) "Cool Offices," *Fortune*, 134 (11), 205–10.

Martin, J. (1996) *Cybercorp. The New Business Revolution*. New York: Amocon.

Salopek, J. (1998) "Coolness is a state of mind," *Training and Development*, 52 (11), 22–34.

Slobodozian, J. (1996) "Networking," *Human Resource Executive*, 20 June, 36–40.

Warner, M. (1997) "Working at home – the right way to be a star in your bunny slippers," *Fortune*, 135 (4), 5.

9

THE STRUCTURE EXCHANGE

Internally focused for externally partnered

M eet Brenda Argosa, owner of three sports and health clubs located in a large suburban community. Brenda has built her enterprise successfully over the last few years by adding new clubs, one at a time, as demand for fitness facilities has grown. She has installed state-of-the art equipment and hired "cream of the crop" athletic instructors and office staff. Brenda has currently experienced an avalanche of new club members and realizes she must add more facilities to capture the business. She begins making plans, calculating the number of staff she will add, the design of a new building, and the equipment she will need to outfit it. She realizes, in order to stay competitive, she should add a nursery and children's program to accommodate the rapidly increasing number of parents within the community this club will serve. She wonders if her food service shouldn't be changed to include a more sophisticated line of organic foods and high-nutrient drinks. She will also need food that appeals to children. Her customer profile suggests many want additional services beyond what Brenda currently provides. Personal training and a wider variety of group classes rank high on her customers' wish list. Besides, she knows the other sports and health clubs in the area provide those services. As Brenda begins to calculate the cost of this expansion, she feels dizzy. Finding the capital to execute the next phase in her business growth seems overwhelming. In her typical, "can-do" manner, Brenda begins to develop a business plan, but the dizziness doesn't go away.

While it may appear that Brenda is moving her enterprise on a fast track to increased performance, she's overlooking some paths to expansion that might allow more effective resource utilization. She seems to be assuming that growth must happen by expanding internally. While independence is the hallmark of entrepreneurs, Brenda may be overlooking some advantages available to her if she considers external partnering. What if she looked around the marketplace for other organizations with which to partner? What existing businesses are highly competent in child care or food service? Could she manage her resources more effectively by forming relationships, even with those health clubs which are now her competitors?

We think greater opportunities for Brenda's company may lie in the concept of partnering.

THE DILEMMA OF USING ONLY INTERNAL RESOURCES TO STRUCTURE YOUR ORGANIZATION

From our interviews we learned that internal expansion alone will no longer cut it. Visionary leaders know that their own resources may not allow them to expand in cost-effective, efficient ways. The high cost of talent, the intense focus on running lean, and the lack of available workers make internal growth less attractive than it once was. Without fully developed resources, organizations will be either in a constant battle to catch up or forced to limit what they do. Neither situation is a good choice because it doesn't stretch the organization to accomplish the max nor does it use the value achieved through economies of scale – all available through the strategy of externally partnering with others.

> *Visionary leaders know that their own resources may not allow them to expand in cost-effective, efficient ways.*

To determine how organizations actually address the dilemma of moving beyond internal structures, we'll tell you what partnering means in several organizations – why and how they do it. Leaders are giving external partnering more credence than ever. Let's explore how through "The structure exchange: internally focused for externally partnered."

STOP DOING THESE THINGS

1 Stop adding to your internal structures alone

To be positioned for the benefits of external partnering, leaders will first need to move beyond a one-sided approach to building their organization. We suggest stopping the intense focus on adding departments, buildings, staff, and miscellaneous resources. Obviously, you shouldn't stop all this because some will be necessary just to keep you in business. What we're most concerned with are those organizations having such an internal focus that they don't consider those opportunities outside their immediate line of vision.

Consider this thought-provoking statement from editor Pam Kruger (1998, p. 214) in a recent issue of *Fast Company*:

> *Say goodbye to the Unit of One . . . Maybe you're starting a new company. Maybe you're leading change in a big company. Whatever your situation, your best resource is a great partner. If you want to go places, you shouldn't do it alone.*

In our interviews we've discovered that internally generated growth, once promoted as the ticket to productivity, is no longer the sole passport to success.

2 Stop thinking your organization has the exclusive rights to its success

According to many leaders we interviewed, thinking that it's only your organization that has a claim to success is a weak position. This reduces your organization's playing field because it doesn't let "outsiders" in to help. Leaders must get outside their cocoons of seeing their successes dependent on everything generated internally.

It boils down to understanding that your organization needs others. You undoubtedly have heard the term "stakeholders" – those individuals or institutions having a "stake" in your success. While we sometimes think of stakeholders as key customers, vendors, or buyers, some stakeholders who are often overlooked are those not directly connected to your business now, but with the right association, could help it be more successful. These are your potential external partners. If you close your mind to their value, you'll unlikely be ready for the external power these partnerships can provide. You can't do it all. And shouldn't!

3 Stop being paranoid about someone stealing your ideas

Let's face it. It's scary thinking of yourself in a position of exposing your creative ideas to others who could potentially take these and run off with them. The threshold of no return is when this vulnerability turns into paranoia. Yes, this could possibly happen. Interestingly, none of the leaders we interviewed reported this occurring! So don't worry excessively that information sharing outside your organization will reduce your strength. We learned it actually has the opposite effect, as you'll soon discover when we explore the "starts".

4 Stop bypassing important partnership considerations

Partnerships should not be developed haphazardly. Would you obtain a mortgage without understanding the terms of the agreement: e.g. interest rate, points assessed, payment schedule? Of course not! Don't enter a partnership without a full delineation of how the arrangement will work. This includes the nuances of partnership initiation, maintenance, and termination.

5 Stop waiting

Leaders have shared with us that trying to do everything perfectly is a tremendous waste of time. While external partnerships require project management skills, you won't need to have every "i" dotted or "t" crossed during the initial exploration of partner building. Waiting for someone else to initiate the partnering process will slow you down and allow competitors to overtake you. Gregg Steinhafel, Executive Vice-President of Merchandising at Target Stores, told us: "Speed is life. Don't do it perfectly; do it today. There's a high sense of urgency. It's too difficult to always pinpoint and define. Get a working prototype out there."

> *Waiting for someone else to initiate the partnering process will slow you down and allow competitors to overtake you.*

Partnering has too many benefits for a wait-and-see philosophy. Their suggestion: stop waiting. Make those initial overtures, the benefits of which we're about to see first-hand when we explore what leaders need to start doing.

6 Stop clinging to weak partnerships

While we're convinced that applying the information that leaders have shared about partnering will increase your probability of success, sometimes partnerships just don't work out. There are times when leaders must stop trying to repair the relationship. When are partnerships too weak to be repaired? If your organization could achieve more individually or with some other partner, then you're ready to focus on ending the partnership. A weak one may stem from a lack of commitment to the relationship on either organization's part. Take note. This may not be bad. It only becomes ineffective if the partner clings too tightly to a relationship that is no longer as productive as one or both of the partners would like. Stay tuned. Later in this chapter we'll tell you exactly what you'll need to do if you find yourself in this situation.

START DOING THESE THINGS

Leaders in many organizations have taken advantage of a full range of external partnerships, helping them expand in successful ways significantly beyond what they could do alone. Those leaders who master the art of working with other organizations will achieve new synergies, have more impact, and create more significance in their work (Hesselbein and Cohen, 1999). Begin with the manageable chunks we outline here under "starts."

1 Start learning the reasons for external partnering

External partnering allows you to grow while streamlining your investment in equipment, resources, research, or development. If your organization is small, partners expand your brainpower by giving you more people with whom to create new ideas. If profit is your motive, then partnering may increase your competitiveness. Non-profit organizations stand to benefit by expanding services when they join forces with others. For many, it is a matter of scale. If you want to make a significant impact in your field, you have to collaborate. Simply put, there is power in numbers.

TCG in Sydney, Australia, has increased its efficiency and agility through masterful partnering. TCG is a group of several dozen companies with a specialization in information technology. It is a clustered network with revenues exceeding $50 million and about 200 staff. Each of the partnered companies claims a competency in such areas as product development, hardware design, and software applications. TCG is structured to make the members more agile than their competitors by their agreements to partner with each other. Specific rules of non-competition apply among member companies with the first and last right of refusal operating.

In interviewing Peter Fritz, Managing Director of TCG, we learned precisely how he structures his external partnerships into "cells," which are actually separate companies, with TCG being the administrative center of the member companies. Each cell provides products and services to member cells within the TCG network and also has its own clients separate from TCG. According to Peter, "A customer is an opportunity . . . either internal or external." The cells are entrepreneurial because each company must have the ability to generate business not only for itself, but also for all of TCG. To many this may sound like any typical corporation with a parent and subsidiaries. There is a major difference. The cells within TCG may exit at will or be asked to exit the network – atypical of a parent corporation with subsidiary companies.

Let's look at another example – three academic institutions – which have created an alliance to expand educational opportunities in their community. The partnership among the University of St Thomas (UST) Graduate School of Business, the University of Minnesota (UM) Carlson School of Management, and the Minnesota Center for Corporate Responsibility (MCCR) allows all three organizations to do more than they could alone. Working together, UST, UM, and MCCR are pooling their research capabilities to shape responsible and ethical business cultures. By doing this, they intend to enhance education of the next generation of business leaders.

2 Start finding suitable partners

Begin with a comprehensive assessment of your organization's capabilities in light of its strategic goals. Then, ask yourself, "Could some of our goals be accomplished more effectively by someone else, given our available resources?" If the answer is "maybe" or a resounding "yes", the search is on.

Our interviewees told us that great partnerships begin with common values and goals. ABB CE Nuclear Power Businesses uses partnering as a key business strategy. Mike Barnoski, President of ABB CE Nuclear Power Businesses in Windsor, Connecticut, said:

> *The key issue in partnering is alignment of goals. In my business, the performance of a plant is key and the top driver is the plant's senior officer. Understanding their goals in partnering needs to fit in with our organization's culture. And once the contract is signed, we get all our employees involved in supporting these goals.*

Mike Stringer explained how Lawson Software pursues goal compatibility with potential partners:

> *To find the right partner . . . we establish expectations [goals] and ask them what they would do to meet them. Most of the time it's not that formal because we have an idea who the right partners are and knock on their doors. At other times we do a formal RFP [Request For Proposal]. We go out to the territory and talk with others in our network and ask them who would be good.*

Effective partners must have capabilities that are complementary to those of your own organization. What can they do that you don't do well or do not have the resources to accomplish? The best partnerships are based on common goals, yet uncommon capabilities. A great example is Arby's and Sbarro – whose partnership has enabled them to be more agile in responding to market forces. Rather than going it alone, the President of Franchise Associates, Inc. (FAI), Charles Nadler, found that the dual-concept restaurant approach could offer customers enhanced dining opportunities. Arby's, which features sandwiches, is more of a lunch occasion and Sbarro, featuring pizza and pasta tends to be more of a dinner occasion. The combination creates great menu variety for FAI's customers and more productive restaurant facility usage for the corporation. At the end of 1998, of the 50 restaurants Franchise Associates manages, 14 were partnered with Sbarro. This concept has allowed Franchise Associates "to continue to pursue significant additional profitable restaurant new store growth" (Nadler, 1998).

As you search for partners, consider making friends with your enemies. We found many examples of partnerships formed among competitors. This approach is particularly effective if both organizations are struggling in some aspect of their business, and can stage a partnership to turn around both enterprises. According to Rick Kusy, Senior Manager at ABB CE Nuclear Power, Nondestructive Examination Services:

> *If you were to have told me just five years ago that we would be partnering with our competitors, I would have asked you to visit your local mental health center and take the MMPI [a psychological assessment instrument]! ABB CE has teamed with companies that were our staunch competitors just five years ago. Now, because utility firms need to be more cost-effective due to deregulation and competition from other power-producing sources, ABB CE is partnering with competitors. No one company can supply the extensive variety of services that utility companies need. In order to reduce their costs, many utilities are combining all the services needed into long-term*

contracts. The services you don't have the capability to produce cost effectively, you team with another company.

Don't forget that a partnership has two sides: theirs and *yours*. What will you have to offer the other party? Will you be a suitable partner to the organization you are romancing? Clearly identify your organization's strengths that may be appealing to someone else. Do you have a particularly successful product or service line which might perfectly complement someone else's? Do you have manufacturing capability others might find attractive? Is your research arm the best in the world? Know what you will bring to the partnership.

Approaching potential partners will require you have a clear set of questions in mind to determine if you have enough in common to further pursue the relationship. Sound like going on a first date? In a way, you are. Box 9.1 provides some questions to ask in the "courting" stage.

➤➤ BOX 9.1   **Questions to determine partner compatibility**

1 Does the capability of this potential partner complement our organization's skills?

2 Do we have compatible values related to quality, customer/client service, financial management, and staff performance?

3 Do we have mutual goals that can be obtained more effectively through a partnership?

4 Does a careful cost-benefit analysis indicate we can gain more by partnering than working alone?

5 Given our mutual goals, what can we offer this partner?

6 How likely is the potential partner to want what we have to offer?

7 How many resources (e.g. financial, staff, equipment) are both parties willing and/or capable of committing to the partnership?

8 What legal parameters will we need to consider if we enter into a relationship with this partner?

9 What proprietary information would we have to share with our partner? Are we willing to and how would we handle it?

Use these questions to determine if a potential partner is a good candidate.

---

3 Start disclosing weaknesses

Don't be afraid to put your cards on the table, exposing what you're not so good at. Expect your partner to do the same, and if you note significant hesitation, back off before it's too late. Partnerships break down when skeletons emerge from the closet too late in the relationship to prevent disaster. Remember. One of the key reasons for creating a partnership may be to compensate for one another's weak points. We are not suggesting you spill your guts. Simply admit your vulnerabilities in the areas most relevant to the partnership.

4 Start constructing a strong foundation

Once you've latched on to a partner, the hard work begins. The most successful partners spend long hours together, even before they tackle the business at hand, hashing out what they're trying to do together and exactly how they will collaborate. They talk about *how* they are going to work together before actually rolling up their sleeves.

Begin with a clear statement of the partnership goals. Ask yourself, "How will we know we have achieved these goals? What will be the measure of success by which we will evaluate our effectiveness?" Then, clarify roles, focusing on who has the relevant expertise, not on titles. The partner who has the majority share of the work usually takes the lead. Examine what each partner can contribute and negotiate the best ways for them to deliver it. Your goal is ultimately to function like a fine-tuned machine. Rick Kusy of ABB CE Nuclear Power told us:

> *Everything should appear seamless to the buyer, in this case the utility firm. If the utility has a problem with something that one of the partner companies is supplying, the utility firm goes to the lead partner, not the company they're having the problem with.*

Another example from Doz and Hamel (1998) is the output coordination and process integration used by Airbus. Daimler-Benz Aerospace in Hamburg works on the internal cabin, with Aerospatiale in Toulouse doing the final airframe assembly, partnering with an array of subcontractors producing airframe sections. Airbus teams with representatives from all major partners conduct flight testing in a coordinated process.

Next, make sure you've identified how you will make decisions together. Determine what each party can do alone and what must be brought before both partners for discussion and group decision-making. Differences in speed of decision-making between each partner organization can be a source of conflict. Smaller, more entrepreneurial partners may become frustrated with the potential sluggish processes of larger, more bureaucratic partners (Doz and Hamel, 1998).

Throughout this process, keep "win-win" in mind. Remember, in a partnership, no one wins unless everyone wins. Conger (1998) identifies these collaboration strategies:

- Establish credibility by showcasing both your specialized expertise *and* effective relationship-building skills.

- Understand the concerns of others and show them how what you have to offer can benefit them.

- Provide evidence that what you're saying is accurate.

- Listen actively; avoid dominating the discussion.

5 Start building and maintaining the partnership

Once constructed, the surest way to maintain the partnership is through ongoing communication. Set up a schedule of meetings to review partnership progress and problem solve issues as they arise. Mike Stringer spoke of how Lawson Software does it:

> We maintain our partnerships through regular communication. We need to understand what they're doing and how they feel about the relationship, and vice versa. The worst thing you can do is nothing once they're signed up. They need to know they have a sponsor who is looking out for the well-being of the relationship. It is tactical, as well – keeping them updated regarding new initiatives, new products, organizational changes. You need to review regularly the return that each party is getting because what will kill it quickly is if one partner is not getting a return any more.

Some partnerships ensure ongoing communication by selecting a representative from each organization to coordinate meetings and information exchange. Their roles might be to inform key partnership players of internal problems cropping up and provide status updates. The critical communication variable is to orchestrate the information flow, not let it happen too randomly.

Expect to disagree. In fact, encourage it. Most successful partnerships our interviewees told us about cultivated their differences. By challenging one another's positions, they develop more creative ideas and sharpen their thinking. However, good partnerships establish ground rules for how to fight fairly and respectfully.

As the partnership matures, you might discover the communication actually drops off. Many partners who succeed in creating mature relationships find they no longer feel a need to concur on every decision. They have less drive to be updated and informed. Why? Because they have come to trust one another. Once you are sure your partner is fully committed to your joint goals and operates with common values, you can relax. The partnership has reached the high performance stage wherein things happen quickly and competently with less interaction.

Refer to Box 9.2 for a summary of what to talk about to build a solid partnering relationship.

>> BOX 9.2 | **Discussion points for building the partnership relationship**

1 Clearly state your joint goal and how you will measure success.

2 Define roles and responsibilities. Decide who will be in charge.

3 Develop your decision-making process. What can partners decide alone and what should be brought to the group?

4 Outline your communication strategy. What information should be shared with whom? How? When?

5 Determine how you will resolve differences.

6 Outline legal parameters for operating the partnership, if relevant. For example, will you create a joint financial entity? How will equity be shared?

Get your partnership started on a firm foundation. Use these discussion points as an agenda for your first few partnership-building meetings.

---

6 Start knowing when to end the partnership

There may come a time when you'll need to say good-bye. We don't pretend to be the Dr Laura of business relationships, advocating that you should stick it out through thick and thin. This is business and sometimes you simply have to cut your losses.

Kruger (1998) identifies four warning signs a partnership may be in trouble. First, if you or your partner's priorities have dramatically changed, the foundation of the partnership may crumble. Second, it may still be working but the stress of interaction outweighs the benefits. You aren't having fun anymore. Third, you may fully enjoy the people involved in the partnership, but they aren't holding up their end of the deal. Time to say "adios." Finally, you or your partner might get a better offer. Another suitor arrives on the scene and sweeps one of you away. Should this occur, try to leave on good terms. You never know when an opportunity might come to reunite.

Establish an adequate mechanism to evaluate how well the partnership is working. Meet periodically with one purpose in mind: discuss whether both parties are satisfied with the partnership. Satisfaction should be measured by how well each party believes the mutually established goals have been accomplished. If goal attainment has not been realized, consider dissolving the partnership. Mike Barnoski told us, "At ABB, the partnership ends when it is no longer of mutual benefit."

You may also find that it's time to end the relationship if the partner organization is no longer fulfilling its side of the bargain. Perhaps the partnership became a low priority or market forces shifted and the arrangement is no longer viable. A breach of the agreement may constitute grounds for divorce.

Before closing the door on a partnership, you might consider mediation. Find an objective individual or team to help you negotiate when problems occur. If this doesn't work, arbitration can be the next level of intervention.

If you get burned by your first attempt at partnering, don't let this experience sour you on trying again. Leaders emphasized to us that partnering is too valuable to toss out due to one unsuccessful attempt. In fact, they stressed that while you're licking your wounds, your competition might be outpacing you by high-powered partnering.

For a complete synopsis of "The structure exchange: internally focused for externally partnered," refer to Box 9.3.

>> BOX 9.3 **The structure exchange: internally focused for externally partnered**

Stop	Start
1 Adding to your internal structures alone.	1 Learning the reasons for external partnering.
2 Thinking your organization has the exclusive rights to its success.	2 Finding suitable partners.
3 Being paranoid about someone stealing your ideas.	3 Disclosing weaknesses.
4 Bypassing important partnership considerations.	4 Constructing a strong foundation.
5 Waiting.	5 Building and maintaining the partnership.
6 Clinging to weak partnerships.	6 Knowing when to end the partnership.

Now, we'd like you to see external partnering in action through a personal profile of expert partner-builder Mike Stringer. What we hope you'll extract from this interview are the day-to-day practices of a leader successfully engaging in external partnering.

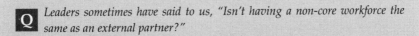

LEADER PROFILE

An expert partner-builder

Mike Stringer
Senior Vice-President, Adaytum Software
(formerly Vice President, International and Alliances,
Lawson Software)

No ordinary leader, Mike has carefully crafted his organization's structure to incorporate external partnering as a key strategic maneuver. While at Lawson Software he positioned the company to be nimble, flexible, and growth-oriented.

Q *Leaders sometimes have said to us, "Isn't having a non-core workforce the same as an external partner?"*

A It is very different. Your non-core workforce is really the area that is outsourced. But it's not the kind of external partnering that we're talking about here. In true external partnering, both parties have a goal in

➤ mind and invest in achieving the rewards of the goal. In outsourcing, one organization provides a specialized service to an area within your business. This is different from external partnering in which there is an external goal that both organizations try to achieve together.

Q *What do you look for in your external partners?*

A The first thing that an organization needs to do is to step back and look at what you're really trying to accomplish. There's a whole spectrum of partnerships and what you're looking for depends on the kind of relationship you're seeking. One major type of partner – *the selling partner* – is one who helps you sell more by providing better product coverage or expanding the product. The second major type of partner is the *customer satisfaction partner*.

Specifically, here are the various types of selling partners:

Co-marketing partnerships occur when two companies decide together to have a stronger value proposition to the market rather than going it alone singularly. Together, they talk about what they can bring to the market. This could include development work to integrate the product better. Let's take an example in healthcare. We provide accounting software. The partner provides the scheduling. If we go to the market together, we can present a bigger solution for the customer – this is what we call having a stronger "value proposition." We work together. If we close the deal, we give our partner some compensation, which we call "revenue sharing" or "spiff." If the partner closes the deal, they share the spiff with us. In this relationship, what we look for is an organization that has a solution to expand the product to give better coverage or penetration in the market.

A twist of the co-marketing partnership is the *agent relationship*. Here, the title of our product is actually sold to someone else. They get a commission when they sell this to their client. What we look for in this partnership is an organization that can credibly sell our products. You have to be careful here that the organization represents you the way you want because your brand is the most important thing you've got.

A VAR (*value-added reseller*) is actually a marrying of two products into something that is truly integrated; they sell the whole bundle. One example of this is the STAR (*strategic territory-affiliated reseller*) which is geographically specific. We look for an organization that can deliver the whole product to the customer in a specific territory. An example of a VAR (not geographically specific) is "Intel" or "Microsoft Office 95" which appears inside your computer. We look for those who can credibly represent the product, sell it, and implement effective solutions.

In an ISR (*industry specific reseller*), there is no geographic specificity. It would be a company that offers such things as billing services to staffing agencies. This is a very specific niche. They take this product and integrate it with the financial solutions we offer. They have a specific solution integrated to that marketplace, and combine it with our generic product. Either they resell it or we do. What we look for is someone who has experience in a specific industry and who can tie this to our application.

At the very opposite end of the spectrum from our selling partner is our OEM (*original equipment manufacturer*) partner. In this relationship, our brand is hidden by the manufacturer. For example, within your computer you can have a disk drive that could be made by Seagate, but you wouldn't know this. In an OEM, we look for a partner who can provide volume and penetration in a market that we have no other way to access.

We build alliances with two kinds of customer satisfaction partners. A *service provider* is typically a partner that focuses on either technical or contract programming. What this really means is that they focus on very specific activities like modifying our software, integrating it with other systems within the client company, upgrading software, or converting it for a customer. It is event-specific. All this helps us achieve our vision. What we look for in the service provider partner is someone who's technically competent in our product. They have to be certified using our tools. We also look for partners skilled in the relevant technologies out there.

An ECP (*enterprising consulting partner*) is a second type of customer satisfaction partner like major consulting firms. They run the main process implementation for a client. They link their skills in process re-engineering with our product and make the client company more effective. The goal here is a quick return on investment for the customer. In an enterprising consulting partner we look for a strong brand or image in the marketplace. We leverage off that. And we also look for someone who can invest in the skillsets around selected products of Lawson.

Q *How long do these partnerships last?*

A With every relationship we put into place, we never have an end date in mind. I would hope they last forever. The reality is that it may not last because of a change in the initial goal. In general, we have had some partners last over 10 years. There are also some relationships that haven't lasted longer than it took for the ink to dry on the contract. Typically, it's at least 12 to 18 months.

Q *How do you establish a partnership?*

A For some, it's very casual and you just have a boiler plate and no attorneys involved. In general, what we do is consider: the purpose of the relationship; the territory or boundary of the relationship; the product or service; the length of the relationship and if it's automatically renewed. We have found that our measure of success does not depend upon a legion of attorneys working on the partnership. But, sometimes, especially around intellectual property rights, you really do need an attorney.

Q *How do you know when to end the partnership?*

A In one scenario there may be a specific breach. This can be anything from fraud to misrepresentation to the partner going out of business. Another way is that one of the two parties is not receiving the value that they wanted or expected. This is more often the case. Partnerships also end when your business changes and you no longer need your partner – you can now do it yourself. When it becomes a low priority for both organizations, it terminates itself because no one is working on it anymore.

Q *Do you ever partner with a competitor?*

A Yes. A great example is Oracle. They have a term called *co-opetition*. They offer a set of products that's similar to ours. But they have a set of data-base technologies which is a stand-alone group of products different from ours. You need this to run a specific application. So we partner with them to help sell their data-base products. But we also compete with their accounting application technology with the same account! This model works but it's definitely not ideal because it creates too much concern and chaos with the relationship.

We also partner with what we call fringe competitors. We just struck up a relationship with one of the biggest healthcare software suppliers in the world. Their whole product is so much bigger than ours. They compete with us with just a very small piece of what we deliver. This is a great competitor partnership.

Q *What kind of bottom-line results have you seen in your external partnerships?*

A If you don't have "skin" [the dollars you invest] in the game the bottom line is pretty low. It's too easy to walk away from the partnership. Where you put more skin in the game you have more of a vested interest in the result. You'll work harder to be successful. Let's take enterprising consulting partnerships, for example. We measure the success in currency: license revenue. But we look for wins for *both* partners. If Lawson wins and the other partner doesn't, we don't count this. It's got to be a win for both partners. In general, the enterprising consulting partnerships impact 40 to 45 percent of our business. Essentially, we've grown by 45 percent per year for the last five years, based upon our work with these partnerships.

Q *Any suggestions for leaders who are thinking of partnering?*

A Yes, get out there and do it! If you don't, your competition will.

REFERENCES

Conger, J. (1998) "The necessary art of persuasion," *Harvard Business Review*, 76 (3), 82–95.

Doz, Y.L. and Hamel, G. (1998) *Alliance Advantage: The art of creating value through partnering*. Boston: Harvard Business School Press.

Hesselbein, F. and Cohen, P. (Eds) (1999) *Leader to Leader: Enduring insights from the Drucker Foundation's award winning journal*. San Francisco: Jossy-Bass.

Kruger, P. (1998) "It takes two," *Fast Company*, Issue 19, 212–26.

Nadler, C. E. (1998) "Frontier days to a fanatical future," Franchise Associates Ink, July 2.

GOING INTO ACTION

R emember the case study in Chapter 1 of Megan Angeles, Vice-President of Marketing for a food company, who was engaged in outmoded leadership practices? Let's look at part two of the case study. Megan has now made significant changes in her leadership approach. Her office is smaller, yet fully equipped with state-of-the art technology for communicating with her virtual staff. By combining more non-core staff with her core team members, she's built a powerhouse of talent, including a cracker-jack ad agency for special assignments. She's ditched the formal job descriptions and created performance contracts for everyone, anticipating their roles will change as market conditions vary and the organization adapts. While Megan has maintained a team structure, she now thinks of her group as one big talent pool and orchestrates project teams more fluidly on an as-needed basis. Project team leaders have the power to make decisions with their team members, while Megan plays the role of advisor and coach.

Many staff work from remote sites, coming into the office periodically. So she's established several team suites comprised of caves and commons along with a few free addresses for temporary usage; few immobile cubicles remain. Additionally, office decor has been transformed: comfy seating arrangements are scattered here and there; videoconferencing facilities have been installed, with video PC fast on its heels; and ping-pong tables provide an arena for fun. She recently led an organizational effort to get a cybercafé built in the main office site.

She has announced many career-building opportunities for staff: sabbaticals, lateral assignments, and team leadership rotation. She's footing the bill for staff attendance and presentations at major conferences, working steadfastly to put the department in the national limelight. She hired a couple of generation Xers who are true mavericks, creative and somewhat irreverent, to challenge her thinking and help everyone keep an open mind. She also brought on two late-career contract staff – traditionalists – to help establish a wider network of relationships with the customer base.

In developing new products, she has worked with the project teams to look for partners – manufacturers of other products which could be paired with her company's food products to craft something new. This vice-president has done a masterful job of *Fast Forward Leadership*. She's stopped her outmoded ways and replaced them with more up-to-date practices. Now she's positioned to lead her organization into the new millennium.

What about you? The journey we have taken you on throughout this book has introduced you to many innovative leaders and told you about their approaches. We have a few additional strategies to motivate you to go into action, just as Megan has done. Here's the problem. How many times have you gone on a trip that brought new experience and insight, causing you to resolve to look at life in a different way? Perhaps you spent a relaxing two weeks on the beaches of Maui and, on the return flight, vowed to yourself never again to get so stressed as you were when the vacation began. Yet how often have you returned to the demands of your everyday existence to find you never quite made the changes you intended? As an outcome of our journey with you through *Fast Forward Leadership*, we don't want this to happen. To prevent slipping back into your former habits, you'll need an action plan to post in your daily planner, near the computer, on your laptop, or in the bathroom – wherever you will see it often and be reminded of the promises you've made to be a better leader.

FAST FORWARD LEADERSHIP
SELF-ASSESSMENT CHECKLIST

Begin to create your personalized action plan with a hard look at your current way of leading. We have designed a checklist (Box 10.1) that is a summary of key behaviors we've suggested in this book and critical to leader success. Grab a writing utensil, sit in a comfy chair, put up your feet, and think about how you would evaluate yourself. Rate yourself a strong "three" on those items you are steadfastly trying to implement in your work unit or organization. If you still have substantial work to do on a particular leadership practice, and are giving it a moderate amount of attention, give yourself a "two." "Ones" go to those items you know need serious work. Then prioritize practices you want to change and jot them down on the "Going into action plan" form we've provided in Box 10.2. We recognize you may not always be the final decision-maker in your organization. Yet you can use your influence with the groups you are part of, as well as in your own leadership arena, to bring these ideas to life. While constructing your action items, don't go overboard in quantity. Begin with no more than three actions and add more as you achieve success and gain confidence.

> ➤➤ BOX 10.1   *Fast Forward Leadership* **self-assessment checklist**

Indicate the extent to which you are engaged in the following *Fast Forward Leadership* practices, by writing the appropriate number in the box after each item:

3 = I am doing this extensively
2 = I am doing this to some degree
1 = I am not doing this.

The communication exchange

Within the organization and/or unit I lead, I am working toward:

- thinking of each communication I engage in as persuasive, not only informative; ❏

- developing my ability to utilize adeptly technological tools for better communication; ❏

- instituting communication standards to manage information dissemination; ❏

- utilizing an array of decision-making approaches that involve others, helping them own issues; ❏

- listening often to a wide variety of people; ❏

- providing training for staff members to help them develop cross-cultural sensitivity. ❏

The workforce exchange

Within my organization and/or unit I lead, I am working toward:

- eliminating obsolete job descriptions; ❏

- reducing the number of full-time, permanent staff; ❏

- determining the type of non-core staff that best meets our staffing needs; ❏

- recruiting non-core staff as carefully as core staff; ❏

- orienting non-core staff as fully as core staff; ❏

- actively managing non-core staff performance, coaching them with regular feedback. ❏

The recognition exchange

Within my organization and/or unit I lead, I am working toward:

- understanding the key differences among generation Xers, baby boomers and traditionalists; ❏

➤

- utilizing a range of strategies to motivate generation Xers; ❏
- utilizing a range of strategies to motivate baby boomers; ❏
- utilizing a range of strategies to motivate traditionalists; ❏
- requiring staff to respect individual uniqueness. ❏

The team exchange

Within my organization and/or unit I lead, I am working toward:

- reducing segmentation between work units; ❏
- decreasing the number of stable, permanent teams; ❏
- creating virtual teams, spanning geographical boundaries; ❏
- developing virtual team-leader skills; ❏
- developing virtual team-member skills; ❏
- utilizing fluid team structures by selecting members from anywhere in the organization; ❏
- combining core and non-core staff, customers, and/or vendors within teams; ❏
- disbanding teams when their usefulness is outlived; ❏
- instituting reward systems that support collaboration. ❏

The development exchange

Within my organization and/or unit I lead, I am working toward:

- choosing team assignments carefully for maverick staff members; ❏
- developing a work environment that stimulates creativity; ❏
- giving maverick staff freedom, but with appropriate boundaries; ❏
- buffering maverick staff from organizational barriers to their effectiveness; ❏
- developing rewards tailored to maverick staff needs; ❏
- reducing any tendency to hire to the status quo exclusively. ❏

The workplace exchange

Within my organization and/or unit I lead, I am working toward:

- developing virtual office capability; ❏
- creating telecommuting opportunities; ❏

- installing appropriate virtual office equipment; ❏
- adapting the main office site with more flexible, mobile furniture; ❏
- adding pizzazz, e.g. recreational areas, work-out facilities, interesting furniture and work spaces, and cybercafés; ❏
- integrating just-in-time, on-call learning capability; ❏
- ensuring the work environment is set up in an ergonomically correct manner; ❏
- giving up any notion that staff must be frequently seen in order to be effectively managed. ❏

The structure exchange

Within my organization and/or unit I lead, I am working toward:

- understanding the reasons for external partnering; ❏
- finding suitable partners, when appropriate; ❏
- encouraging openness to disclosing organizational weaknesses in order to make a partnership work; ❏
- instituting a process for forming partner relationships by clarifying goals, responsibilities, and decision making processes in the early stage of partnership formation; ❏
- maintaining a partnership through ongoing communication; ❏
- maintaining a partnership through ongoing problem solving; ❏
- knowing when to end a partnership that is not working effectively. ❏

Scoring interpretation guide

If your rating was:	It suggests:
Mostly 3s and 2s	You are in a class of innovative leaders, utilizing updated and emerging practices. Pat yourself on the back.
Mostly 2s and 1s	While you show some glimmers of updated leadership practices, you are at risk of slipping further behind. Increase the speed with which you are implementing new methods.
Mostly 1s	Begin at once to overhaul your leadership practices to avoid loosing effectiveness. Treat the situation as urgent.

>> BOX 10.2 **Going into action plan: top priority exchanges**

Three Fast Forward Leadership *practices I want to begin or strengthen*	*Action steps to make it happen*	*Completion date*

CONSIDER THE WORDS YOU USE

Now that you've reviewed the principles of *Fast Forward Leadership* as they relate to your own leadership approach, there is one more finishing touch we'd like you to consider. It is most likely clear by now that the traditional vocabulary leaders use may not fit the fast-changing conditions of organizational environments. For example, do you find yourself saying things like, "That proposal will have to go up the chain in order to get approval," or "The boss won't be pleased when she hears this," or "The workers will need to be informed." Each of these phrases contains verbiage that doesn't entirely fit the new ways of work life. It represents the old hierarchical, rigid structures, which are fast becoming relics of another era. To help make sure you don't give mixed messages as you employ *Fast Forward Leadership*, we have given you one last set of "stops" and "starts" in Box 10.3 which delineates vocabulary you should eliminate from your repertoire and what to say instead. You may be surprised at how much of leadership jargon you hear and read hasn't been edited to fit changes in organizational culture.

►► BOX 10.3 The leadership vocabulary exchange

Stop using these terms	*Use these instead*
Upper management	Central management
Supervisor or boss	Team leader Coach Leader
Worker or employee	Staff person Team member Partner Owner (for stock ownership) Associate Producer Talent
Chain-of-command or hierarchy	Decision-making process
Job	Work
Job description	Performance contract
Office	Workspace Virtual environment
Promotion	Lateral opportunity

RATCHET-UP YOUR COOLNESS

For those of you who may be feeling like you can't quite keep abreast of newly emerging phraseology, consider expanding your vocabulary by integrating some terms that will allow you to participate more fully in jargon-ridden dialogue. These are terms of the technology age, and while not the most cutting edge, will give you a way to communicate with those who use this new vocabulary. If a colleague said to you, "Let's hire her; she's plug-and-play," how would you respond? If a staff person complained about a colleague who was "busy signaling," would you know what they were talking about? What if another leader asserted your corporate competitor's new product was just "vaporware"? Could you carry on a dialogue without struggling to understand? The glossary of essential vocabulary at the end of this chapter will allow you to be hip with the times (whoops!), rather cyber-savvy.

CONTINUE THE JOURNEY

As we've said in this book, learning should be a part of your daily life, integrated into all you do. Think of yourself as both a teacher and learner as you go forward with *Fast Forward Leadership* in mind, using the following strategies to keep yourself and others ahead of new developments.

Track trends and adjust accordingly

Think about this. The "starts" we've laid out in this book will eventually become the "stops," as new leadership behaviors become more appropriate for the next phase of your organization's development. Here lies your opportunity to become, if you are not already, one of the next generation of innovative leaders we hope to interview for the next edition of this book.

Develop insight by studying trends – economic, political, social, and demographic – affecting the world today and predicted to have impact in the future. Read broadly outside your professional field. The most innovative leaders often have multiple interests, many not related to the work they do. They create new ideas by exposing themselves to information uncommon to their professions. Then, like a twist of a kaleidoscope, they reformulate the information to apply it to their own organizations.

Consider taking an assignment outside your field

To immerse yourself further in new ways of thinking, consider an entirely different work assignment. As we discussed in the "recognition exchange," career development in these times means lateral movement and growth through new experiences. Why not apply this to yourself, not only to those you lead? What if you took a sabbatical and worked in another part of the world, increasing your multi-cultural sensitivity? What if you exchanged places with another leader in your organization or somewhere else? What if you changed professions entirely, applying your skills, for example, to a non-profit organization if you currently work in a corporation? A "shake-it-up" approach may be just what you need to get your mind racing with new vision.

> *A "shake-it-up" approach may be just what you need to get your mind racing with new vision.*

Consult with others of a different generation and culture

To expand your awareness, as well as your ability to relate, find a person or two who is not a member of your own generation and someone of a different culture, then make them part of your network. A development concept we like, called the "Personal Board of Directors," entails making a list of people with whom you want to develop relationships, each for different reasons. The goal of this group is to give you the mentoring, support, teaching, and cheerleading you need to develop yourself fully. They are your advisors. Make sure the Board of Directors you assemble includes multi-generational membership. Assuming we can only learn from those older than we are is an archaic thinking pattern. Form professional alliances with those younger people who have expertise you want to acquire. Include multi-cultural representation, as well, to challenge any stereotypical biases you may harbor and to give you a global view.

Find innovative leaders to model

Search your organization, and elsewhere, to find innovative leaders who can serve as your role models. Exploit the value of vicarious modeling – learning by observation. For example, have you ever gone to another country and come back with a slight accent, even if your trip was only for a few days? You acquired the behavior, just by exposure. Surround yourself with people who have the talents you would like to have. Watch them carefully, observing the nuances of their behavior and the response it elicits from others. Increase the amount of interaction you have with these leaders and see what rubs off.

Share the learning

Use this book as a guide to teach others. If you're not teaching, you're not leading. While you're busy finding your own sages, be aware that others are looking to you to be their coach. Distribute what you've learned via staff meetings, e-mail, newsletters, in individual coaching sessions, or on your Web site. Don't hoard the information you've acquired, but rather, spread the power that comes with knowledge acquisition. Remember that this is the era of the learning organization, when leaders must think of every interaction they have with their staff, and others, as an education opportunity.

Find time for self-reflection

As you learn more about your leadership approach, you'll naturally discover the things you are good at, as well as what challenges you. Work hard to alter behaviors that inhibit your ability to provide good leadership, but we don't advise you to completely overhaul your personality. The best leaders we know are keenly aware of their strong suits and weaknesses, searching out situations in which to lead that are a good match for their strengths and minimizing exposure of their less desirable traits. Good leadership occurs when the interaction between the leader's characteristics and the situation in which they work is a good fit. Know what you are good at. Find the optimum environment that allows those traits to shine. Then, surround yourself with others who complement and supplement your talents. Select members of your team who are *not* your clones.

A FINAL WORD

We hope you've discovered some new ways to think about leadership and are ready to go into action, refreshed from the journey and energized to become the best leader you possibly can. If you want to be better at something, you can't just read or talk about it. You must make the commitment to change your behavior, taking on more challenges over time to grow stronger. High performers develop through tough assignments they are often not fully prepared for. So, here is our assignment for you: do something differently because you've read this book. Be an even better,

> *You must make the commitment to change your behavior, taking on more challenges over time to grow stronger.*

more innovative leader than you are now. Implement *Fast Forward Leadership*.

ESSENTIAL VOCABULARY

Alpha geek The most knowledgeable, technically proficient person in an organization. "Ask Jane, she's the alpha geek around here" (Cohen,1996).

Bandwidth The capacity to take on additional work, similar to an older phrase, "stuff on my plate." As in, "Right now I don't have the bandwidth to do that."

Bitnik Someone who uses a coin-operated computer terminal in a coffee house to log on to cyberspace (Cohen, 1996).

Blendo A combination of different media, including graphics, scanned images, animation, and text; a multimedia approach, also called "meltomedia" (Cohen, 1996).

Busy signaling Rapid hand movements indicating what the person on the telephone is saying is more important than what colleagues want to interrupt you with (Branwyn, 1998).

Chips and salsa Chips = computer hardware, salsa = computer software. "Let's see if the problem is in your salsa or your chips" (Branwyn, 1994b).

Coin-operated employees An employee brought in for a given project for a specified period of time (Branwyn, 1998).

Collocation Positioning of individual and teamwork settings in sufficient proximity to one another to allow productive interaction. The rule of thumb is a distance of no more than 50 feet (*Fast Forward*, 1996).

Commons Flexible open space with movable furniture and whiteboards for impromptu meetings. This may be combined with the "hearth," where employees can use the fax and copy machines, get coffee and mail, eat, look at periodicals, access their personal storage space, and schmooze (*Fast Forward*, 1996).

Co-opetition Co-operating with a business competitor in order to improve the performance of both organizations.

Cybrarian A person who makes a living doing on-line research and information retrieval. Also know as a "data surfer" or "super searcher" (Cohen, 1996).

Dawn patrol Programmers who, when you return the next morning, are still at their computers (Branwyn, 1994a).

Desktop videoconferencing (DVC) The capacity to hold videoconferences on desktop (or laptop) computers.

Drop-in or just-in-time office An office used in turn by numerous employees.

Enclave A private room or office that is checked-out for a period of time.

Empowerment *(not what you think!)* Having the necessary equipment to link up other employees. After installing new technology for a staff person, you might say, "He's empowered, now."

Face time Time spent face-to-face with clients.

Free address A workspace shared on a first-come, first-served basis.

Geeksploitation Taking advantage of generation Xers who are willing to work long hours if given enough junk food, flexible schedules, and no dress code (*Modern Maturity*, 1997).

Group address A group or team space that is designated for a period of time. It is not permanent.

Group decision support systems Computer-based information systems used for group decision making. They allow groups connected via a local area network and software to generate, organize, and rank ideas.

Groupware Software that allows many people to share information and resources, manage data, and communicate via group conferencing and e-mail. It may also include features like scheduling and project management.

Harbors and commons Privates spaces and shared meeting rooms.

Hot desking Several people using the same desk at different times.

Hotelling Off-site offices set up for shared, temporary use.

Off-site Out of the office.

Mindshare Similar to the concept of "market share." Used to refer to the amount of interest something captures. As in, "This concept grabbed a lot of mindshare."

Mission critical Essential to get a job done.

Mobile A service or salesperson who spends most of the time out of the office.

Mouse potato A computer addict (*Readers Digest*, 1997).

Non-territorial offices A workspace in which individual staff members no longer have assigned desks or workstations.

Plug-and-play Refers to a new staff member who doesn't need any training. "The new guy is great. He's totally plug-and-play."

Snail mail The US postal service.

SoHo Acronym for Small Office, Home Office (Branwyn, 1994a)

Technographer A meeting facilitator who utilizes computer-based decision-support systems.

Vaporware A new product announced before it is developed that ultimately is not developed (*Reader's Digest*, 1997).

Virtual office The freedom to office anytime, anyplace created through the use of technological tools.

Work process What staff do, how they do it, when they do it, where they do it, and the tools they use to do it (*Fast Forward*, 1996).

Note: Our thanks to Dr Susan Lund for her help in preparing this glossary. Dr Lund is profiled in Chapter 6, "The Team Exchange".

For the most recent jargon, read Gareth Branwyn's regular feature "Jargon watch" in Wired magazine.

REFERENCES

Branwyn, G. (1998) "Jargon watch," *Wired*, 6 April, 48.

Branwyn, G. (1994a) "Jargon watch," *Wired*, 2 February, 31.

Branwyn, G. (1994b) "Jargon watch," *Wired*, 2 June, 31.

Cohen, S. (1996) "Cool sites," *Training and Development*, 50 (10), 20.

Fast Forward (1996) August, 2.

Modern Maturity (1997) "Youth watch," 40w (5), 26.

Readers Digest (1997) February, 56.

INDEX
·····················